IRISH DÁIL AND SENATE 1922—72

SOUTHAMPTON UNIVERSITY STUDIES
IN PARLIAMENTARY PAPERS

A SELECT LIST OF REPORTS OF INQUIRIES

OF THE

Irish Dáil and Senate
1922–72

P. and G. FORD

REF

IRISH UNIVERSITY PRESS

ISBN 0 7165 2254 3

Irish University Press, 81 Merrion Square, Dublin 2

PRINTED IN THE REPUBLIC OF IRELAND

CONTENTS

ACKNOWLEDGEMENTS

For the assistance and information they gave us in response to our queries we wish to give our warm thanks to Mr Liam Carbury, Librarian of the Dail; Mr B. O Brolchain, the Controller, Eire Stationery Office; Mr Brian McKenna, National Library of Ireland; Mr K.A.C. Parsons, Cambridge University Library; Mr Blake, London School of Economics Library; Mr E.J. Miller, British Museum; Mrs Lewy; and especially to Mr Sean Browne, Irish University Press. We wish to thank Miss Marshallsay for preparing the index.

SCOPE AND ARRANGEMENT

The aim of this Select List of Eire Papers is to help students to follow the development of thought on Eire's main lines of domestic policy since the foundation of the State. With few exceptions, it is therefore confined to the Reports of inquiries, White Papers, etc., on policy in constitutional, economic, social and legal matters. The List is thus in a broad sense arranged by subject fields, and is not a chronology, though in each field chronology has its place. Where the topic of a paper spreads into more than one subject we have sometimes given a duplicate entry, and we have occasionally indicated that the text of a paper is also accessible in the British Sessional Papers.

In the confusion of the times when the State was being fought for and established, papers were issued and circulated in various ways and many of them are now scarce. This List begins when the official Stationery Office Catalogues begin–1922. In view of the specific purpose of the List it does not include Acts of the Oireachtas which followed inquiries, since these can be found in the published bound volumes; but in a few cases when they give significance to a series of papers, fill a gap or indicate a change of thinking which an outside researcher might otherwise miss, they have been entered. Similarly, a large number of 'information' papers, papers concerned with executive action, statistical statements and annual returns of statutory bodies, etc. are not included.

Dates and reference numbers. In books and articles a report may be given one of three dates: the year in which it was signed on behalf of the committee or commission or by the author, the year in which it was officially presented, or the year in which it was published. These are commonly, but not necessarily, the same, though each may have its own historical interest. Many papers do not have the publication date on the cover or the title page. Presented papers have official numbers which are printed on most, but not all of them. These are not given in the catalogues of the Stationery Office, which has its own system of numbering for its task of storing the papers, keeping them accessible and selling them. Students outside Eire are hindered by the fact that collections of Eire Papers—and of catalogues—are often imperfect or scanty, and it therefore seemed best to base the List on the Stationery Office Catalogues, dates and code numbers, by quoting which institutions and researchers can ask for the Papers they want. We have tried to do this consistently and to reduce to a minimum any confusion between presented and publication dates.

Others matters of interest to scholars, such as the forms and methods of inquiries, presentation dates, and official procedures for handling papers, as well as the provision of a substantial guide to their contents, it is hoped to take up in later work. We decided that in the meantime Irish studies would be best furthered by issuing this List as the first stage.

To assist the readers not familiar with them we have provided a short introduction indicating the historical setting in which some of the more significant inquiries took place.

NOTE:

This List is based on Stationery Office code numbers, and does not, except in certain cases, give presented numbers. For other information on presented papers readers can consult the *General Index to the Proceedings of Dail Eireann.*

A glossary of English language equivalents of the Irish language titles and terms will be found in App.III in the Report of the Public Services Organisation Review Group 1966-69.

INTRODUCTION

This Select List of Eire Papers aims at including policy reports of inquiries, White Papers, etc., to be found in the Dail, Seanad, Oireachtas and other Government publications, so arranged as to show the development of thinking on the constitutional, economic, social and legal policies of Saorstat Eireann since its foundation. It is subject to certain limitations and difficulties, but it seemed important to us just now that, outside Eire as much as in it, there should be a fuller understanding of what the policies have been and how they have evolved, and that the official sources of information about them should be more widely known.

Certainly, outside Eire the extent and interest of the material to be found in the papers on the development of the country and its policy is not fully realized. The papers show the unique features of the Irish problem. In the great volume of public, political, business and theoretical discussion on the development of undeveloped countries, attention has been in the main focused on those ex-colonial territories whose population is increasing at an exceptional rate, often much higher than that of the developed ones. But in Eire the whole demographic picture and the problems raised are quite different, for although also an undeveloped country, its population had been declining or little more than stationary and there had been a large net emigration. Again, unlike ex-colonial territories, many of which had varying forms of fairly independent local administration with rudimentary representative elements, Ireland since the Union had been part of a single political unit following unified financial, fiscal, free trade and even social policies which suited the dominant industrial partner, but which were not attuned to the needs of a poor agricultural economy. The policy of free trade, so long the framework within which British industrial expansion took place, was a questionable benefit to Ireland, except to the north-eastern industrialized corner. The Royal Commission of 1895-96 on the *Financial Relations between Great Britain and Ireland* and the Primrose Committee of 1911-12 on *Irish Finance* made it clear that Ireland had in various ways been disadvantaged by a financial partnership which compelled it to keep pace in certain types of expenditure with a country several times richer. The cost of the unified postal service rose by seventy four per cent because it meant the provision in Ireland, with seventy per cent of its population living in rural conditions, of postal services on a scale required by Great Britain where only twenty per cent of the population was in rural areas. The charge of old age pensions at the age of seventy required one-third of the true Irish revenue because its population of four millions contained the survivors of a population which seventy years earlier was eight millions.

In the task of breaking out from this situation the new state was faced with many difficulties. The problem was not simply one of separating from the major industrial unit and the development, in a time of peace and steady progress, of policies adapted to the resources, needs and the various ideals so widely canvassed by Irish writers from Plunkett to AE, Darrell Figgis and James Connolly. On the contrary, ways had to be found to deal not only with these long-run problems, but also with more pressing short-term ones—the damage arising out of the war for independence and the greater damage of the civil war, the difficulties of a small agricultural country living within a group of major industrial ones and unable to insulate itself from their ups and downs (such as the Great Depression of the 1930s), from the difficulties of its major market, Britain, or from the effect of the Second World War.

Papers in this List show some of the movement of thought and discussion on how, despite these distractions, the main course should be pursued. In agriculture, whether the aim should be self-sufficiency, which meant more arable and smaller herds, or maximum agricultural employment, or promoting agricultural exports, which involved intensifying pastoral farming. In industry, the first stage was electrification, with the Shannon project; and tariffs, in the beginning selective then general, in order to increase manufacturing for the domestic market, followed by active steps to develop the turf industry and to encourage tourism. There were grants to increase employment in particular areas. Yet by the middle fifties, in spite of progress, circumstances combined to give results which were a disappointment. The rise in productivity was slow and emigration was tending to increase rather than decrease. While some members of the Commission on *Emigration and other Population Problems* (1949-54) wanted to see population increased, the decline of family size and emigration arrested, and the drift from country to town (especially to Dublin) reversed, it emerged from the various reports that a forced cessation of emigration would mean unemployment, a fall in wages and general living standards. A rise of average income was needed to offset the attractions of emigration, and this required increased agricultural and industrial exports at competitive prices. Yet the low density of population and an over-large proportion of the older age groups were themselves a hindrance to expansion. There was therefore a search for a new dynamic. (It is interesting to recall that Robert Owen, in his evidence to the Committee on *Employment in Ireland*, 1823, noted the under-employment of a large part of the population and said that a large Government expenditure on the development of industry was needed.) Should the restrictions on the investment of foreign capital in Ireland, imposed to prevent overseas firms, especially British, from being set up to reap the gains of the tariff, be replaced by encouragement under specific conditions?

From the middle fifties policies begin to take a more positive direction. One conclusion of the Capital Investment Committee, following up suggestions made by Geary, McCarthy and Meenan to the Commission on Emigration, was that over-emphasis on social investment should be corrected by giving greater priority to productive investment. Was the greatest need the release and stimulus of enterprise and capacity—the prohibition of restrictive practices and the encouragement of new methods in technology and management—so that industries could compete efficiently in the international market? The Restrictive Practices Act, 1953, and the Fair Trade Commission were directed to the first, while the reports of the Committee on Industrial Organisation on State aid to industries to enable them to compete in the Common Market, on export marketing, on adaptation councils for individual industries to stimulate rationalization and on a score of individual industries, were concerned with the second. The Papers, from those on *Economic Development* and *Economic Expansion*, 1958, show increasingly the influence of Keynesian theory and concepts. The efforts to deal with particular industries, public and private capital investment, consumption, etc. could be co-ordinated, expansion programmes prepared, targets worked out after full consultation with industries, and achievements periodically checked against them. So Eire, going forward steadily and impressively with the Second and Third Programmes, now moved like other countries into an era of planning and fuller and active participation of Government in the promotion of economic growth. The papers become elaborate statements of economic and social research. As with other countries there were successes and failures, and much to learn; but the papers show an increasing hold on the problems involved.

This process of forecasting and planning and positive State activity involved the creation of new administrative instruments— State-sponsored corporations, boards and companies of many kinds, concerned with commercial activities as varied as promoting tourism, turf production, the marketing of dairy products and of pigs, road and rail transport, the generation of electricity, as well as State-sponsored private companies. The capital requirement of these sponsored bodies amounted to about fifty per cent of total State capital expenditure. The new State took over 21,000 civil servants from the British administration, abolished a large, not very logical array of boards and commissions, and by the Ministers and Secretaries Act, 1924, created eleven functionally organized departments, each under a minister. But the new tasks have called for 34,000 civil servants, 12,000 fee-paid and industrial servants, while there are 60,000 employed by State-sponsored bodies. The massive report of the *Public Services Organisation Review Group*, 1966-69, examined in the light of current administrative and management theory, the function and organization of the various grades of the civil service, the chains of responsibility and the several tasks of each of the departments of State, the goals of State-sponsored bodies, their accountability and audit, as well as the recruitment of their staff and their place in the public service. It was not concerned simply with the recruitment and management of the civil service, as was the Fulton Commission for Britain, but discussed many of the principles and topics covered by the Haldane Committee on the *Machinery of Government*. The order and clarity of the proposals for the allocation of duties to and the structure of the departments compares very favourably with some of the ad hoc politically-motivated changes in British departmental structure in the last few years.

To adapt a phrase sometimes found in early nineteenth-century historical writing, the curtain did not fall in 1921 on the drama of an 'old' Ireland to rise immediately to start an entirely new one. The actors might be new, the themes different, but the audience was the same. The ordinary routine of life takes place within a framework of law, custom, ideas of rights and institutions which cannot be discarded instantly and wholesale without the risk of painful disruptions in everyday life. The interest of some of the papers lies in the light they throw on the decisions about what should be retained, what scrapped and when. To fulfil its task the new regime often made use of the instruments which were lying to hand. The new Constitution, unlike that of Britain, was set out in a basic law, but many British Parliamentary procedures and even terminologies were continued – the Select Committee, the White Paper, Statutory Rules and Orders, Statutory Instruments, etc. Some general and some particular decisions had to be made about the continued validity and enforcement of many laws: those concerning property and contract, for example. For some years minimum wage rates continued to be fixed under the Trades Boards Acts, 1910-18, and occasional inquiries made into wage disputes under the Industrial Courts Act, 1919, until these were replaced by the Labour Court and the procedures provided by the Industrial Relations Act, 1946. Old age pensions, granted under the 1908 Act and such a boon to the recipient, and owing to the age-composition of the Irish population such a strain on the Irish exchequer, had to be continued. Something had to be done about the obligations and division of assets created by the National Insurance Act, 1911 (under which administration of health matters was based on friendly societies) as Irishmen working or resident in various parts of England were members of a large number of Irish societies. And of the 276,000 insured persons in Northern Ireland, 117,000 were members of societies with headquarters in Southern Ireland. Sometimes there had been a cleavage of policy which had to be resolved. The majority of the Poor Law Commission of 1909, in their Report on Ireland, had rejected the proposal for a salaried medical service in hospitals, made by the Vice-Regal Commission of 1906 and largely in effect repeated in 1920 by the Irish Public Health Council. The recommendation of the Departmental Committee of 1908 on *Irish Forestry* (British Sessional Papers 1908 Cd.4027,4028,xxiii) that a million acres of woodland were essential and that a national scheme of afforestation was required, remained the accepted objective. The position of the Irish Land Purchase Acts and the administrative bodies, the Land Commission and the Congested Districts Board, was vital to Irish agricultural and population policy, and it was natural enough that they should be immediately replaced by a new Irish Land Commission. It was generally agreed that the transfer of ten million acres from landlords to tenants, the creation of economically viable units and the erection of cottages had been a great reform. But there remained the problems of educating an ill-prepared peasantry to produce not just for subsistence, but for the market, and of deciding what should be done for the landless for whom no holding could be provided. Moreover the question of whether the annuities collected from these tenant-purchasers should be transferred to Britain or retained by the Irish exchequer occasioned a bitter and damaging dispute between the two countries. How far can a poor peasantry with a low standard of living pay purchase-instalments on top of their rent to any government, British or Irish, until their techniques have been improved? (Compare the huge defaults and cancellations of the Russian peasants' payments on the land transferred to them in the nineteenth-century reforms.) The many papers on agriculture show the immense pains taken to improve methods and marketing.

Two other sets of papers illustrate the problems posed by separation. A new central bank had to be created. How independent of the Government was its management to be? What its relation to other commercial banks? What its part in influencing over-all fiscal, financial and economic policy? The new State started with the advantage that the Boundary Agreement, 1924, freed it from any national debt. But it also began life under British income tax laws. The yield and effect of income tax in an industrial country with growing corporate profits and investment

income, and with wealth very unequally distributed, so that tax
can be graduated to fall more heavily on the higher income levels,
is very different from those of income tax in a poor agricultural
country, faced with deciding how far high rates of direct taxation
would discourage or eat into the savings which were the source of
the capital needed for its development plans.

Finally, there was the Gaeltacht. The revival of the Irish
language, literature and culture—at one time suffering as much
from social denigration as from active Government hostility, and
from the erosion that ordinary commercial intercourse with
Britain seemed to involve—had always been a primary aim of the
Irish nationalist movements. The papers record the many steps
taken to make it the official language, to introduce it into the
public services, and then to revive it as the language of common
speech. Efforts were concentrated on the Gaeltacht where relative
economic backwardness and rural depopulation, threatened its
survival. The restoration of the language thus meant much more
than training new teachers, building schools or providing Irish text-
books. It meant under-pinning the language by the economic
development of the area, reviving traditional industries and trying
to plant new ones.

The papers are a fascinating and well-documented record of the
endeavours of an undeveloped country with a population depleted
of much of its natural increase, trying to raise its standards and to
re-create itself in the light of its own ideals, using old and making
new institutions for the purpose. This List is not intended as a
history, and the papers themselves do not quite tell the whole
story. Some matters of import and of detail were settled in the
light of current views expressed in speeches, writing, the declara-
tions of interested groups and in the debates of the Dail and
Seanad, without being preceded by a particular investigation. On
such matters it is to those sources that the historian must go. But
the creation of a new State on so broad a front touches its
members at every point and involves choices of action over the
whole field of community life. This *Select List* deals with those
reports of inquiries by committees, commissions and other
Government agencies concerned with these matters of policy. A
glance at the List shows how many there were! It is hoped that it
will serve to introduce students to the material they contain on
Eire's problems and policies for its first fifty years.

SUBJECT CLASSIFICATION OF PAPERS

SELECT LIST OF PAPERS

I MACHINERY OF GOVERNMENT

1 Foundation of the State and the Constitution

1922	M.8/1	Draft Constitution of the Irish Free State to be submitted to the Provisional Government 1922.
	/2	—— The English translation.
1922	M.9	Select Constitutions of the world. Prepared for presentation to the Dail Eireann by order of the Irish Provisional Government, 1922, with historical notes and index.
1922	M.7	Correspondence of Mr Eamon De Valera and others.
1922	5/22	Executive articles of the Constitution of the Soarstat Eireann Bill. Dail Cttee. Rep. (T.5).
1922	PP.10/1	Memo on re-draft Constitution. Agreements arrived at between the late President Griffith and Mr Kevin O'Higgins on the one hand and the Southern Unionists on the other. Sept. 1922. (M.1).
1922		Constitution of the Irish Free State (Saorstat Eireann) Act.
1922	2/22	Articles 21 and 23 of the Constitution and suggested appointment and remuneration of officers of the Seanad. Seanad Cttee. Rep. R.2.
1923	1/23	—— Interim Rep.
1922-25	M/12	Handbook of the Ulster Question issued by the NE Boundary Bureau. Illustrated with maps and statistical charts.
1923	12/23	Interpretation Bill. Dail Sessional Cttee. of Selection nominating deputies to serve on a special committee to consider the Interpretation Bill. 2nd Rep. (T.18).
1925	2/25	On matters affecting the interpretation of the Constitution. Seanad Cttee. Rep. R.32.
1922-25	M.10/1	Speech of the Governor General to both Houses of the Oireachtas 12th Dec. 1922.
1922-25	M.6	Property Compensation Commission set up by agreement between the British Government and the Irish Provisional Government. Terms of Reference, 1922.
1924	M.13	Correspondence between the Government of the Irish Free State and H.M. Government relating to Article 12 of the Treaty between Great Britain and Ireland, from 19th July 1923 to 17th June 1924.
1925	PP.19	Agreement supplementing and amending the Articles of Agreement for a Treaty between Great Britain and Ireland. (Articles 12, 5.)
1926	PP.50	Heads of the ultimate financial settlement between the British Government and the Government of the Irish Free State.
1929	R.41	Claims of British ex-service men. Cttee. Rep.
	R.41a	—— Memo on the Rep. of the Cttee. on Claims.

Annex I   *Decrees of the Provisional Government*

1922   1/22   Proof of official documents.
         2/22   Technical instruction (temporary provisions).
         3/22   Army commissions.
         4/22   Unemployment insurance.
         5/22   Finance decree.
         6/22   Unemployment insurance.
         7/22   Restrictions on importations.
         8/22   Restrictions on importations (amendment).
         9/22   Courts—emergency provisions.
         10/22   Criminal injuries.

Annex II   *Some Relevant British Parliamentary Papers*

Some of the Papers relating to the founding of the Irish Free State are very scarce, but can be found in the British Parliamentary Sessional and other Papers. Below is a select list of the more important ones.

Establishment and functions of an Administrative Council of Ireland; 1907 (182) ii 481.

Irish Convention. Rep. of proc; 1918 Cd.9019 x 697.

Government of Ireland Act, 1920.

Proposals for an Irish Settlement. Correspondence relating to; 1921 Cmd.1470 xxix 401: 1921 Cmd. 1502 xxix: 1921 Cmd. 1539 xxix.

Article of Agreement for a Treaty between Great Britain and Ireland; 1921 Sess. II. Cmd. 1560 i 75.

Proposals for an Irish settlement. Correspondence between H.M. Government and the Prime Minister of Northern Ireland; 1921 Sess.II. Cmd.1561 i 83.

Irish Free State (Agreement) Act, 1922.

Irish Free State Constitution Act, 1922 Sess. 2.

Irish Free State Consequential Provisions Act, 1922 Sess. 2.

Provisional Government (Transfer of Functions) Order 1922. S.R.O. 1922. No. 315.

Heads of working arrangements for implementing the treaty; 1923 Cmd.1911 xviii 123.

Irish Free State Consequential Adaptation of Enactments Order 1923. S.R.O. 1923 No. 405.

Irish Free State (Confirmation of Agreement) Act, 1924. [Article 12].

Ireland (Confirmation of Agreement) Act, 1925. [Articles 12,5].

Irish Confirmation of Agreement Act, 1930. [Article 10].

Statute of Westminster 1931.

Boundary Commission. Correspondence between H.M. Government and the Government of the Irish Free State; 1923 Cmd.1928 xviii 123. 1924 Cmd.2155 xviii 69. 1924 Cmd.2166 xviii 97. 1924 Cmd.2264 xviii 113.

Boundary Commission. Rep. of the Judicial Cttee. of the Privy Council as approved by Order in Council, 31st July 1924 on the question connected with the Irish Boundary Commission referred to the Cttee; 1924 Cmd.2214 xi 351.

Compensation Commission. Warrant of appointment; 1922 Cmd.1654 xvii.

Heads of the ultimate financial settlement between the British Government and the Government of the Irish Free State; 1926 Cmd.2757 xxii 115.

Papers relating to the Parliamentary Oath of Allegiance in the Irish Free State and to the land purchase annuities; 1931 Cmd.4056 xiv 273.

2 Constitutional Developments

1926	PP.53	Legislation to amend the Constitution. Certain proposals. Sel. Cttee. Rep.
1927	2/27	Constitution (Amendment No. 5) Bill, 1926. Seanad Sel. Cttee. Rep. R.42.
1927	PP.54	Joint House Oireachtas Cttee. Rep.
1928	PP.59	Constitution of Seanad Eireann. Joint Sel. Cttee. Rep.
1936	R.60/1	Second House of the Oireachtas. Commission Rep.
1935		Irish Nationality and Citizenship Act.
1936		Executive Authority (External Relations) Act.
1937	PP.63/2	Draft Constitution amended in Cttee.
	/3	—— Amended on Rep.
	/4	—— Approved by Dail Eireann.
1937	PP.44/1	Constitution of the Irish Free State (Saorstat Eireann) Act, 1922, embodying the Constitution as amended by subsequent enactments.
1937		Constitution of Ireland Act, 1937 (Dec.24).
1937	2/37	Seanad Electoral (Panel Members) Bill, 1937. Dail Sel. Cttee. Interim Rep. (T.94).
	3/37	—— 2nd Rep. (T.95).
1947	1/47	Seanad panel elections. Joint Cttee. Rep.
1953	2/53	Seanad Electoral (Panel Members) Bill, 1952. Seanad Sel. Cttee. Rep. (T.142).
1959	R.96	Seanad Electoral Law Commission, 1959, Rep.
1968	R.107	Constitution. Rep. of the Cttee. on the Constitution, 1967.

3 Elections

1924	T.11	Names of townlands and towns in Ireland with Parliamentary county or borough in which situated.
1925	3/25	Procedure of triennial elections. Seanad Cttee. Rep. R.33.
1960	2/60	Electoral law. Joint Cttee. Interim Rep. (T.173).
1961	1/61	—— 2nd Interim Rep.
	2/61	—— 3rd Interim Rep.
1962	1/62	—— Interim, 2nd, 3rd and Final Reps.

4 Members

1922	2/22	Salaries and allowances. Pairlimint Shealadach. Dail Cttee. Rep. (T.2).
	3/22	—— 2nd Rep. (T.3).
	4/22	—— 3rd Rep. (T.4).
	2/23	—— Rep. (T.8).
1923	9/23	Dail Sessional Committee of Selection nominating Members to certain special cttees. 1st Rep. (T.15).
	12/23	—— Nominating Deputies to serve on a special committee to consider the Interpretation Bill. 2nd Rep. (T.18).
1926	PP.55	Incapacity for Membership of the Oireachtas. Joint Cttee. Rep. procs.

1948	R.79	Members and the sale of Locke's brewery. See p. 49.
1952	2/52	Question of the effect of Senator William McMullen's bankruptcy on his Membership of the Seanad. Seanad Cttee. of Procedure and Privileges. Rep. (T.125).
1962	1/62	Amendment to Standing Orders relating to suspension of Members from the service of the Dail. Cttee. Rep. (T.185).
1949	3/49	Members fund. Dail Committee of Procedure and Privileges. Rep. (T.126).
1960	3/60	Scheme for contributory pension for Members. Joint Cttee. Rep. (T.175).

5 Procedure

1922	2/22	Articles 21 and 23 of the Constitution and suggested appointment and remuneration of officers of the Seanad. Seanad Cttee. Rep. R.2.
1923	1/23	—— Interim Rep. See p.18
1922	1/22	Standing Orders. Pairlimint Shealadach. Dail Cttee. Rep.
1923	3/23	Procedure. Dail Cttee. Rep. (T.9).
	4/23	—— 2nd Rep. (T.10).
	5/23	—— 3rd Rep. (T.11).
1924	7/24	Procedure in regard to Seanad amendments to bills. Dail Joint Cttee. Rep. (T.24).
1927	1/27	Procedure. Seanad Cttee. 1st Rep. (R.41).
1930	1/30	Procedure relative to Standing Orders. Seanad Cttee. Rep. R.50.
1930	2/30	Procedure relative to Standing Orders. Seanad Cttee. Rep. R.51.
1930	PP.14/2	Standing Orders relative to public business. Seanad Cttee. Rep.
1946	2/46	The subject matter of bills to consolidate statute law. Dail Procedure and Privileges Cttee. Rep.
1949	4/49	Amendment to Standing Orders relating to notice of questions. Dail Proc. and Priv. Cttee. Rep. (T.127).
1966	1/65	Amendment to Standing Orders relating to notice of questions. Dail Proc. and Priv. Cttee. Rep. (T.127).
1923	10/23	Private bill procedure. Joint Cttee. Rep. (In Dail Reps.) (T.16).
	11/23	—— 2nd Rep. (T.17).
1924	PP.10/3	Procedure in the case of private bills. Memo. Leas-Chathaoirleach of the Senate. Mar. 1924.
1924	13/24	Private Bill Costs Bill. Seanad Sel. Cttee. Rep. R.27.
1936	5/36	Private Bill Standing Orders. Dail Sel. Cttee. Rep. (T.92).
1953	2/53	Private Members' motions. Amendment to Standing Orders relating to time limit to debate on Private Members' motions. Dail Proc. and Priv. Cttee. Rep. (T.141).
1959	1/59	Private Members' motions. Standing Orders relating to the time limit to debate. Dail Proc. and Priv. Cttee. Rep. (T.168).
1924	8/24	Private business No. 40 of the Standing Orders relative to private business. Joint Cttee. Rep. (In Dail Reps.). (T.25).
1924	13/24	Matrimonial matters. Standing Orders (private business) on the position in Saorstat Eireann on bills relating to matrimonial matters. Joint Cttee. Rep. (T.30).

1932	PP.15/2	Private business. Standing Orders of Dail and Seanad relative to private business. Cttee. Rep.
1958	3/58	Private business. Standing Orders on the amendments of the Standing Orders relative to private business. Joint Cttee. Rep. (T.165).
1956	1/56	Ruling by the Cathaoirleach on an amendment to the Local Government (Superannuation) Bill. 1955. Seanad Proc. and Priv. Cttee. Rep. (T.153).
1961	1/61	**Amendment of Standing Orders. Dail Proc. and Priv. Cttee. Rep. (T.182).**
1962	1/62	Standing Orders. (i) Amendment to Standing Orders relating to suspension of Members from the services of the Dail. (ii) New Standing Order relating to order of motions in Private Members' business. Dail Proc. and Priv. Cttee. Rep. (T.185).

6 Privileges

1934	2/34	Exclusion of certain duly authorised visitors. Seanad Cttee. Rep. R.57.
1947	1/47	Fracas between two Members of the Dail, 24th April 1947. Dail Cttee. Rep. (T.119).
1949	1/49	Statements relating to a Member made by a Minister in the Dail Dec. 14 1948. Dail Cttee. Rep. (T.120).
1952	1/52	Assault committed by a Member on another Member in the Oireachtas restaurant 31st Jan. 1952. Dail Cttee. Rep.
1953	4/53	Premature disclosure of a report of a Dail Sel. Cttee. Rep. (T.143).
1956	1/56	Newspaper article in sporting press. Dail Cttee. Rep. (T.155).
1970	3/70	Magazine item containing criticism of Ceann Comhairle.

7 Officers of the House

1922	2/22	Articles 21 and 23 of the Constitution and suggested appointment and remuneration of officers of the Seanad. Seanad Cttee. Rep. R.2.
1923	1/23	—— Interim Rep.
1929	1/29	Remuneration of the Cathaoirleach and Leas-Chathaoirleach Seanad Special Cttee. Rep. R.47.
1946	3/46	**Wearing gown by Ceann Comhairle. Dail Proc. and Priv. Cttee. Rep.**
1946	4/46	—— Additional Rep.
1951	1/51	Provision for contingency where both Clerk and Clerk-assistant of the House are absent. Seanad Proc. and Priv. Cttee. Rep. (T.131).

8 The House: Accommodation

1923	7/23	**Accommodation of the Oireachtas. Joint Cttee. Rep. (In Dail Reps.)**
1924	5/24	Temporary accommodation of the Oireachtas. Joint Cttee. Rep. (In Dail Reps.) (T.23)
	10/24	—— 2nd Rep. (T.27).
1928	PP.57	Joint Restaurant Cttee. Rep.

1929	1/29	—— 2nd Rep. (T.53).
1930	2/30	—— 3rd Rep. (T.63).
1931	2/31	—— 4th Rep. (T.70).
1932	1/32	Joint Restaurant Cttee. Rep. (T.76).
1934	1/34	—— Rep. (T.80).
1935	3/35	Oireachtas restaurant. Future of management. Joint Sel. Cttee. (T.83).

9 Ministers

1922	6/22	Committee elected to nominate Ministers who shall not be Members of the Executive Council. Dail Rep. (T.6).
1923	8/23	—— Cttee. Rep. (T.14).
1930	1/30	Remuneration of Ministers and the allowances of Members of the Oireachtas. Joint Cttee. Rep. (T.61).
1935	R.64/1	Ministerial and other salaries etc. Cttee. Rep.

10 Departments

1924		Ministers and Secretaries Act.
1924	R.30	Army Inquiry Cttee. Rep.
1926	R.31	Ordnance survey. Cttee. Interim Rep.
1971	175/67	Labour (Transfer of Departmental Administration and Ministerial Functions) Order 1967. S.I.

11 Civil Service

1923	1/23	Appointment of Controller and Auditor General. Dail Cttee. Rep. (T.7).
		Civil Service Commission:–
1936	R.54/2	—— Final Rep. with apps. Vol.I.
	/3	—— Interim and Final Reps. apps. Vol I.
	/4	—— Memos. of ev. Vol II.
	/5	—— Memos. of ev. Vol III.
1965	F.68	Post-retirement adjustment in public service pensions. Cttee. Rep.
1966	F.73	Rates of remuneration payable to clerical recruitment grades in the public sector. Tribunal of Inquiry.
1969	F.81	Public services organisation. Review group. 1966-69 Rep.

12 Local Government and Finance

1926	R.32	Greater Dublin Commission Rep.
1938	R.66/1	Local Government (Dublin) Tribunal Rep.
1937	1/37	Local Government (Galway) Bill 1937. Dail Sel. Cttee. Rep. (T.93).
1945	K.44	Powers and functions of elected Members of local bodies.
1953	PP.56/23	Local Government Bill 1952. Special Cttee. Debate. D9.
	/24	—— Special Cttee. Rep. (T.136).
1965	K.83	Planning and Development Act, 1963. Explanatory Memo.
1971	K.103	Local government re-organisation.
1970	K.102	Use of computers in local government.
1971	K.104	Local Authority Engineering Organisation. Rep. to the Minister of Local Government. (Clerkin Rep.).

1930	1/30	Local Authorities (Officers and Employees) Act, 1926. Dail Sel. Cttee. Rep. (T.62).
1956	1/56	Ruling by the Cathaoirleach on an amendment to the Local Government (Superannuation) Bill, 1955. Seanad. Proc. and Priv. Cttee. Rep. (T.153).
1969	K.100	Higher remuneration in the public sector. Review body. Rep. to the Minister of Local Government on findings of Local Authority Officers Arbitration Board on claims by Local Authority Engineers and County Accountants. 26th Sept. 1969.
1931	R.43	De-rating Commission. Reps.
		Local Finance and Taxation. Inter-Dept. Cttee. Reps:—
1965	K.86	—— Valuation for rating purposes.
1967	K.93	—— Exemption from and remission of rates.
1968	K.93/1	—— Rates and other sources of revenue for local authorities.

13 Delegated Legislation

For list of Reports of Seanad Committee on Statutory Rules and Orders, Regulations and Statutory Instruments, see Stationery Office Lists.

II NATIONAL FINANCE

1923-24	R.20	Fiscal Inquiry Cttee. Reps.
1925	R.24	Taxation of road vehicles. Road Advisory Cttee. Sub-Cttee. Interim Rep. Feb. 1925.
1926		Tariff Commission Act.
1927		Tariff Commission. For reps. see p. 27
1925	1/25	Public Accounts Cttee. Rep. T.33. See succeeding Reps.
1926-28	PP.45/1	Double income tax. Agreement between the British Government and the Government of the Irish Free State
	/2	—— Explanatory Memo.
	/3	—— Agreement 25th April 1928.
1946	PP.28	Supplies and Services (Temporary Provisions) Bill, explanatory Memo.
1956	R.85	Taxation on industry. Cttee. Rep. Pr.3512.
		Income Tax Commission. Mr Justice O'Dailaigh (Ch).
1959	R.92	—— 1st Rep.
	R.92/1	—— 2nd Rep.
1960	/2	—— 3rd Rep.
	/3	—— 4th Rep.
1961-62	/4	—— 5th Rep.
	/5	—— 6th Rep.
1962-63	/6	—— 7th Rep.
1959	F.60	Income tax. A new system for the taxation of salaries and wages.
1962	F.61	Direct taxation. White Paper. Pr.3952.
1967	1/67	Consolidation Bills on the income tax. Standing Joint Cttee., Rep. 1966. (T.210).

| 1967 | | Income Tax Act. |
| 1971 | | Proposals for a value-added tax. White Paper. Prl.1721. |

Capital Investment Advisory Committee:—

1957	F.53/1	—— 1st Rep.
1958	/2	—— 2nd Rep.
	/3	—— 3rd Rep.
1965	F.71	Public capital expenditure. Pr 8562.

III MONEY AND MONETARY POLICY

		Banking Commission 1926. Professor H. Parker-Willis *Ch.*
1926	R.33/1	—— 1st Interim Rep. Banking and currency, 1926.
1926	/2	—— 2nd, 3rd, 4th, Interim Reps. on agricultural credit, business credit and public finance.
1927	/3	—— Final Reps.
1927		Currency Act.
1929	3/29	Bank of Ireland Bill 1929. Jt. Cttee. Rep. PB.4.
1929	4/29	—— Certain amendments. Rep. PB.5.
1935	1/35	Bank of Ireland Bill 1935. Jt. Cttee. Rep. (T.82).
1933		Industrial Credit Act.
1938	R.63	Banking, currency and credit. Commission 1938.
1937	R.63/1	—— Mins of ev. Vol. I.
1938	R.63/2	—— Mins of ev. Vol. II.
1942		Central Bank Act.
1971	R.112	Banks inquiry. (Fogarty Report).
1932	2/32	Moneylenders Bill 1929. Dail Sel. Cttee. Rep. (T.74).
	5/32	Moneylenders Bill 1932. Dail Special Cttee. (T.78).
1926		Coinage Act.
1928	F.27/1	Currency Commission year ending 31.3.28. Ist Ann. Rep. (See succeeding Ann. Reps.).
1929	F.31	Coinage of Saorstat Eireann 1928.
1960	R.97	Metric system and decimal coinage. Cttee. Rep. 1959.
1961-62	E.48	The earliest Irish coinage. W. O'Sullivan M.A. D.Econ.Sc.
1965	F.69	Decimal currency. Working party. Rep.
1968	F.79	The new Currency System. Irish Decimal Currency Board. Bulletin No. 1.
1969	F.84	Irish Decimal Coinage Board. 1st Ann. Rep. 1968-9. (See succeeding Ann. Reps.).

IV AGRICULTURE AND FOOD

1. General Policy, Land Commission, Land Purchase.

| 1922/25 | M.50/1 | A description of soil-geology of Ireland based on geological survey, maps and records with notes on climate. J.R. Kilroe. |
| 1931 | A.19 | Facilities for advanced study and research in agricultural science and cognate pure sciences in the Irish Free State. |

1958		Agriculture (An Foras Taluntais) Act.
1959	A.44	Survey of agricultural credit in Ireland. Fred. W. Gilmore (Deputy Governor U.S. Farm Credit Administration).
1964	A.54	Agricultural co-operation in Ireland, Joseph G. Knapp. An appraisement.
1967	A.59	A review of the Irish agricultural advisory service. Rep. by Mr W. Emyrys Jones and Mr Albert J. Davis.
1922	L.1	Irish Land Commission. Rep. year ending 31st March 1921.
1922-25	L.7/1	Congested Districts Board of Ireland. 29th & 30th Reps. years ending March 1921, 1922.
1922-25	L.6	Estates Commissioners' Rep. Year ending March 1921 and for 1903-21.
1922-25	K.10	Labourers (Ireland) Order, 1906.
1923	27/23	Land Laws (Commission) Act, 1923. An Act to amend the law relating to the Irish Land Commission and to dissolve the Congested Districts Board for Ireland and transfer its functions to the Irish Land Commission.
1929	L.1/3	Irish Land Commissioners' Rep. for the period ending April 1923 to March 1928 and prior period 31st March 1923. (See succeeding ann. Reps.).
1926	PP.43	Land Bill 1926. Memo.
1926	PP.52	Land Bill No. 2 1926. Sel. Cttee. Rep.
1933	R.47/1	Sale of cottages and plots provided under the Labourers (Ireland) Act. Comm. Rep.
1931	F.33	Land purchase annuities. Attorney General. Memo. P.569.
1932	X.11/2	Land purchase annuities. Text of notes between the Government of the Irish Free State and the British Government.
1936	1/36	Land Purchase (Guarantee Fund) Bill 1935. Ruling of Cathaoirleach. Seanad. Proc. and Priv. Cttee. Rep. R.59.
1935	PP.61	Land Purchase (Guarantee Fund) Bill, 1935. Reps. and Procs. of the Priv. Cttee. under Article 35 of the Constitution.
1936		Labourers Act, 1936.
1899		Agriculture and Technical Instruction (Ireland) Act.
1902		Department of Agriculture and Technical Instruction (Ireland). 1st General Rep. British Sessional Papers; 1902 Cd.838 xxv.
1907		Provisions of the Agriculture and Technical Instruction Acts. Dept. Cttee. Rep., Ev., etc: British Sessional Papers; 1907 Cd.3572, xvii; Cd.3573, Cd.3574, xviii.
1923-24	R.25	Agriculture. Commission. Reps.
1932	A.1/10	Department of Agriculture and Technical Instruction for Ireland. 29th Rep. and Final Rep. 1930-31.
1933	A1/11	Agriculture. 1st Ann. Rep. of the Minister for 1931-2.
1944-45		Post Emergency Agricultural Policy. Cttee. T.A. Smiddy (Ch).

1944	A.31/1	—— 1st Interim Rep. Cattle and dairying industries.
	/2	—— 2nd Interim Rep. Poultry production.
1945	/3	—— 3rd Interim Rep. Veterinary service.
	/4	—— Final Rep. Pr.7175.

| 1946 | A.36 | Policy in regard to crops, pastures, fertilisers and feeding stuffs. |

| 1948 | | European recovery programme. Ireland's long term programme, 1949-53. Pr.9198. |

1949	A.38	Present state and methods for improvement in Irish grasslands. Rep. 1949. G. A. Holmes, M.Sc. P.9248.
1965	122/4	Agricultural Statistics 1960.
1962	I.110	National farm survey, 1955-6—1957-8, Final Rep. Pr.6180.
1961-62	A.52	Problems of small western farms. Rep. Pr.6540.
1964	A.52/1	Problems of small western farms. Inter-Dept. Cttee. Rep. on pilot area development. Pr.7616

| 1964 | A.55 | Agriculture in the second programme for economic expansion. Pr.7697. |
| 1970 | A.65 | A review of State expenditure in relation to agriculture. Cttee. Rep. |

| 1970 | A.64 | Irish agriculture and fisheries in the E.E.C. Prl. 1085. |
| 1971 | A.67 | Agriculture in the west of Ireland. |

2 Particular Products

| 1921 | R.10/3 | Stock breeding farms for pure-bred dairy cattle. Rep. (See Resources and Industries p. 31) |

| 1922 | R.10/9 | Dairying and dairy industry. Rep. (See Resources and Industries p. 31). |

| 1924 | 12/24 | Dairy Produce Bill. Dail Special Cttee. Rep. 1924. (T.29). |

| 1931 | A.18/1 | Marketing of butter. Tribunal. Interim Rep. |

| 1931 | R.36/9 | Butter. Application for a tariff. Tariff Commission Rep. 9. |

| 1946 | A.34 | Guaranteed market and prices for dairy produce. Rep. 9. White Paper. |

| 1961 | | Marketing of Irish butter in Britain. White Paper. Survey team. Min. of Agric. Pr.6333. |

| 1963 | A.53 | Dairy products industry. Survey team. Rep. Pr.6960. |

| 1968 | A.61 | Irish dairy organisation (Cook and Sprague). |

| 1928 | K.25 | Milk supply. Advice as to cleanliness and wholesomeness. Inter-Dept. Cttee. Rep. |

| 1947 | K.50 | Milk supply for the Dublin sale district. Tribunal of Inquiry. Rep. |

| 1967 | A.60 | Two-tier milk price. Study group. Rep. |

| 1933 | R.48/1 | Pig industry. Tribunal. Interim Rep. |
| 1934 | /2 | —— Pig production in Soarstat Eireann. |

| 1932 | R.36/14 | Bacon, hams and other pig products. Tariff Commission Rep. No. 14. |

| 1935 | 2/35 | Pigs and Bacon Bill, 1934. Dail Special Cttee. Rep. (T.81). |

| 1939 | R.52/5 | Price charged for bacon including hams and gammon. Prices Commission. Rep. of investigation. |

1938-40		Agriculture. Commission.
	A.30/1	—— 1st Interim Rep. Pigs and bacon industries.
	/2	—— 2nd Interim Rep. Silage.
1946	A.35	Reorganisation of the pig and bacon industries. White Paper.
1963	A.53/2	Bacon and pig meat industry. Survey team. Min. of Agric.
1963	A.53/1	Beef, mutton and lamb industry. Survey team. Min. of Agric. Pr.6993
1969	A.62	Store cattle. Study group. Rep.
1958	R.91	Glenamoy grass meal project. Cttee. Rep. 1958.
1925	A.8	Poultry industry, Dublin. May 1911, Conference. Rep. of Proceedings.
1962	A.51	Broiler industry (Poultry Products Council). Rep.
1963	A.51/1	Turkey industry. Rep.
1964	I.115	Poultry Inquiry Rep. 1960-1.
1943	R.73/1	Fruit and vegetables. Tribunal. Rep.
1970	I.131	Fruit and vegetables processing industry. Cttee. on Industrial Progress.
1966	A.58	Glasshouse industry. Survey team. Min. of Agric. and Fish.
1931	R.44	Grain Inquiry. Tribunal Rep.
1929	R.42	Wheat growing and a question of a tariff on flour. 1st and 2nd Interim Rep., Economic Cttee. 1928.
1934	R.52/1	Wheaten flour. Investigation into prices charged. Prices Commission. Rep.
1958	R.89	Milling and baking. Quality of Irish wheat. Institute of Industrial Research and Standards. Interim Rep. covering 1956 harvest.
1965	A.56	Study of wheat standards and the marketing of wheat in Ireland. Rep. by Dr Robert Olered.
1965	A.53/4	Provender milling industry. Survey team. Min. of Agric. Rep.
1965	A.53/3	Oatmeal milling industry. Survey team. Min. of Agric. Rep.
1966	A.53/5	Flour milling industry. Survey team. Min. of Agric. Rep.
1935	R.57/1	Horse breeding industry. Commission, Rep.
1966	A.53/6	Horse breeding industry. Survey team. Min. of Agric. & Fish.
1924	A.5/1	Diseases of Animals Acts, with Returns of the imports and exports of animals for the year 1920. 1st Ann. Rep., Rep. of Proceedings. (See succeeding Ann. Reps.)
1934	1/34	Slaughter of Animals Bill, 1933. Dail Cttee. Rep. R.56.
1970	I.101/40	Conditions which obtain in regard to the supply and distribution of bovine hides and skins. Fair Trade Commission. Rep.
1966	A.57	Wool improvements. Cttee. Rep.
1970	A.63	Mushroom industry. Survey team. Min. of Agric. & Fish.

| 1966 | I.122 | Fertiliser Prices Inquiry. Prices Advisory Body (Fertilisers) Order, 1965. Rep. |
| 1930 | 3/30 | Game Preservation Bill, 1929. Conference between Members of the Dail and the Seanad upon Amendment No. 6 made by the Seanad. Rep. (T.65). |

3 Export Marketing

Advisory Committee on the Marketing of Agricultural Produce. Reports: Dr J. Greene *Ch.*

1959	A.41	—— Export of bacon and other pig meat. Pr.5082.
	A.42	—— Export of shell eggs and liquid eggs.
	A.43	—— Export of turkeys. Pr.5393.
	A.45	—— Export of dairy produce. Pr.5236.
	A.46	—— Export of live stock and meat. Pr.5224.
	A.47	—— General aspects of Irish export trade in agricultural produce. Pr.5225.
	A.48	—— Poultry other than turkeys. Pr.5271.
	A.49	—— Export marketing of Irish agricultural produce. Pr.5225.
	A.50	—— Turkey export trade, 1959, Pr 5120.
1970	X6.447	Supply of bacon to the United Kingdom market. Memo.

4 Forestry

1908		Irish Forestry. Dept. Cttee. Rep., evidence, in British Sessional Papers; 1908 Cd.4207, Cd.4208, xxiii.
1949	X.22	Agriculture in the long term programme. Pr.9198. (See Papers on economic expansion.)
1951	L.58	Forestry mission to Ireland. Food and Agriculture Organisation of the United Nations. Cameron Rep. Feb., 1951. Pr.664.

5 Drainage

1925	W.2	Regulation of the River Barrow drainage. Rep. Professor E. Meyer-Peter, Zurich.
1925	W.3	River Barrow drainage. Rep. T. M. Batchen, M.I.C.E.
1925	5/25	River Owenmore Drainage Bill. Seanad Sel. Cttee. Rep. R.35.
1930	W.5	Lough Erne drainage. Rep.
1928	K.28	The Arterial Drainage (Minor Schemes) Regulations, 1928.
1929	4/29	Arterial Drainage (Amendment) Bill. Dail Special Cttee. (T.59).
1941	R.68/1	Drainage Commission, 1938-40. Rep.
1961	W.6/1	River Shannon flood problem. 1st stage of investigations 6th June 1961. Rep.

6 Fisheries

	G.1	Proposed whaling stations in County Donegal. Rep. of inquiries held in 1908.
	G.3/3	Trawling grounds on the coast of Counties Down, Louth, Meath, Dublin. Part I. Record of fishing operations. E.W.L. Holt. Survey, Rep. 1909.
	G.3/2	Fishes of the Irish Atlantic slope. 4th Rep. E. W. L. Holt and L. W. Byrne. 1908 No.V.
	G.3/4	—— 5th Rep. 1910 No.VI.

1927	G.8	Sea Fisheries Conference. Rep.
1931	1/31	Sea Fisheries Bill, 1930. Seanad Special Cttee. Rep. R.52.
1935-37	R.35/1	Inland Fisheries Commission. Rep. 1933-35.
1956	2/56	Fisheries (Statute Law Revision) Bill, 1956. Seanad Special Cttee. Rep. (T.157).
1960	G.15	Development of sea fisheries industries. Rep.
1962	G.17	Programme of sea fisheries development.
1962	G.13/9 13/10	Foyle Fisheries Commission Reps.
1962	G.16	Project for improvement of the fishing harbour facilities. Rep. C.G. Bjuke.
1964	G.18	Improvement of the sea fisheries of Ireland. Recommendations by an American survey team. Pr.7983.
1966	G.21	Irish fisheries investigations. Series A. (freshwater) No.1-7.
1970	A.64	Irish agriculture and fisheries in the European Economic Community. Prl.1085.

5 ECONOMIC EXPANSION AND PLANNING: TRADE AND INDUSTRY

1 Resources and Industries

Resources and industries of Ireland, 1920-22. Commission of Inquiry. Reports:

1920-22	R.10/1	—— Milk production. Mar. 1920, Interim Rep.
	/2	—— —— In Irish.
	/3	—— Stock breeding farms for pure dairy cattle. April 1921. Rep.
	/4	—— Coalfields of Ireland. Memoir July 1921 Vol.I. Maps. Vol.II.
	/5	—— Sea fisheries. Oct. 1921. Rep.
	/6	—— Peat. Dec. 1921. Rep.
	/7	—— Industrial alcohol. Dec. 1921. Rep.
	/8	—— Waterpower. Jan. 1922. Rep.
	/9	—— Dairying and dairy industry. Mar. 1922. Rep.
	/10	—— —— In Irish.
	/11	—— —— Milk production and milk products—Fishery.
	/12	—— Minutes of evidence Part II. Co-operative organisation—meat trade—coal—water—power—peat—industrial alcohol—mineral resources—harbour development.
1922	M.50/2	Localities of minerals of economic importance and metalliferous mines in Ireland. Memoir and map. Grenville A.J. Cole, F.R.S.,M.R.I.A.
1924	M.50/3	Barytes in Ireland. T. Hallissy, B.A., M.R.I.A., F.G.S.
1944	I.81/1	Irish mineral resources. A short review. T. W. Bishop, A.R.S.M., F.G.S.
1944	I.81/2	Geological Survey of Ireland. Pamphlet No. 2. Irish sources of limes and magnesia of high purity, limestone, dolomite and brucite marble.
1944	I.81/3	Geological Survey of Ireland Emergency Period. Pamphlet No.36. Sources of industrial silica in Ireland.

1952	I.98	Industrial potentials in Ireland. An appraisal. I.B.E.C. Technical Services Corporation.
1966	I.124	Science and Irish economic development. Main Rep. Vol.I.
	I.124/1	—— Vol. II. Appendices.
1969	F.85	Research and development in Ireland, 1967.

2 Electrification

1922	I.12	Water power resources of Ireland. Sub-Cttee. Rep. 1921.
1922	R.10/8	Water power. Rep., Jan. 1922.
1924	I.13/1	Proposed hydro-electric scheme on the River Shannon. Correspondence between the Ministry of Industry and Commerce and Siemens-Schuckert werke, Berlin.
1925	I.13/2	The electrification of the Irish Free State. The Shannon Scheme developed by Siemens-Schuckert.
1925	I.13/3	The Shannon scheme. Reports by experts appointed by the Government.
1929	5/29	Electricity Agreements (Adaptation) Bill, 1929. Dail Special Cttee. Rep.
1944	I.13/4	Rural Electrification. Rep. prepared by the Electricity Supply Board 1944.
1959	R.87	Atomic Energy Cttee. Rep. 28th May 1958.
1966	I.123	Electricity in Ireland. Scope of agreement on cross-border co-operation.

3 Tariffs, Excise. Control of External Investment in Ireland. Anglo-Irish Trade

1926		Tariff Commission Act.
		Tariff Commission Reports:
1927	R.36/1	Application for a tariff on rosaries.
	/2	—— Margarine.
1928	/3	—— Flour.
1929	/4	—— Woollens and worsteds.
	/4a	—— Woollens and worsteds, supplementary Rep.
	/5	—— Down quilts.
	/6	—— Fish barrels.
1930	/7	—— Packing and wrapping papers and cardboards.
1931	/8	—— (i) An increase in the tariff on bodies of motor vehicles. (ii) The imposition of a tariff on (a) the bodies of certain mechanically propelled or hauled vehicles and (b) vehicles intended for animal traction.
	/9	—— Butter.
	/10	—— A modification of the tariff on woollens and worsteds.
	/11	—— Leather.
	/12	—— Oats.
1932	/13	—— Linen piece goods etc.
	/14	—— Bacon, hams and other pig products.
1934	/15	—— Book of prayer.
1939		Tariff Commission Repeal Act.
1926	R.29	Importation of motor parts. Inquiry into delays of clearance. Cttee. Rep.

1932-34		Control of Manufactures Acts.
1958		Industrial Development (Encouragement of External Investment) Act.
1967	F.77	Accession of the Government of Ireland to the General Agreement on Tariffs and Trade (GATT). Pr.9694.
1926	PP.46	Home grown tobacco duties. Special Cttee. Interim and Final Reps., Procs., Mins. of ev., apps.
1926	2/26	Home grown tobacco duties. Dail Special Cttee. (T:39).

Anglo-Irish Trade:—

1965		Free Trade Area Agreement. White Paper Pr.8625.
1966	F.66/11	Comments on the Free Trade Area Agreement. N.I.E.C. Pr.8610.

The text of agreements on Anglo-Irish Trade can be found also in British Sessional and other Papers as follows:—

1937-38	Agreement between the Government of the United Kingdom and the Government of Eire. 1937-8 Cmd.5728,xxx.
1937-38	Copy of the United Kingdom-Eire Trade Agreement (Commencement) Order 1938; 1937-8 Cmd.5748,xxx.
1947-48	Trade Agreement between the Government of the United Kingdom and the Government of Eire; 1947-8 Cmd.7504,xxix.
1965-6	Agreement between the Government of the U.K. and the Republic of Ireland establishing a Free Trade area between the two countries, Dec. 1965; 1965-6 Cmnd.2858,xvi.

4 Prices, Cost of Living Index

1923	R.15	Prices. Commission. Rep. July 1923.
1922-23	I.15/1-14	Cost of Living. Reps. June 1922 to mid-Oct. 1925.
1927	R.37	Prices Tribunal. Rep.
1933	R.46/1	Cost of living index figure. Cttee. Rep. 1932. Pr.992.
1934	R.51/1	Shops. Commission on Registration. Rep.

Prices Commission. Investigation into prices charged. Reps:

1934	R.52/1	—— Wheaten flour.
1936	/3	—— Bread.
1937	/4	—— Batch bread.
1938-40	/5	—— Bacon, including hams and gammon.
1935	R.52/2	—— Bodies of mechanically propelled vehicles.
1937		Control of Prices Act.
1951	R.81	Flour and bread inquiry. Interim and Final Reps.
1954	I.104	Household budget inquiry. 1951-2. Pr.2520.
1969	U.104/1	Household budget inquiry. 1965-6.
1958		Prices Act.

5 Turf

1921	R.10/6	Peat Rep. see Resources and Industries p.31.
1936		Turf (Use and Development) Act, 1936.

Industrial Research Council:

1937	I.58/1	—— Trials on industrial heating appliances using turf as fuel. Bull. No. 1.
1942	/2	—— Turf as domestic fuel. No. 2.
	/3	—— Irish peat waxes. No. 3.
	/4	—— Turf as fuel for steam boilers. No. 4.
1946	I.84	Turf development programme.
1946		Turf Development Act.

6 Tourism

1940	I.79/1	Irish Tourist Board 1st Ann. Rep. 1940.
1946	I.86	Tourist development programme.
1951	I.95/1	Synthesis of reports on tourism, 1950-1.

7 Merchandise Marks, Fair Trading

Merchandise Marks Commission. Reports:

1934	R.50/1	—— Modern furniture.
	/2	—— Playing cards.
	/3	—— Tags made of paper, manilla or cardboard.
1969	/4	—— Ceramic ware.
	/5	—— Aluminium holloware and containers and electric kettles.
	/6	—— Biscuits.
1970	/7	—— Vitreous enamelled ware.
	/8	—— Plumbers' brass foundry and compression couplings.
	/9	—— Stockings, socks and the like.
	/10	—— Men and boys outer garments.
	/11	—— Proposals to amend the Merchandise Marks (Restriction on Importation of Ceramic Ware) Order. 1969.
1970	I.129	—— Knitted and crocheted clothing.
	/1	—— Carpets.
	/2	—— Footwear.
	/3	—— Jewellery.
1953		Restrictive Trade Practices Act, 1953.

Fair Trade Commission. Reports:

1955	I.101/12	—— Radio sets and accessories.
1955	/13	—— Building materials and components.
1956	/16	—— Motor vehicles, tyres and other parts and accessories.
	/17	—— Grocery goods and provisions.
1957	/20	—— Proprietary and patent medicines and infant and medical and toilet preparations.
1958	/26	—— Operation of the Restrictive Trade Practices (Motor Cars) Order.
1959	/27	—— Operation of the Restrictive Trade Practices (Radios) Order.
1960	/29	—— Carpets, carpeting and floor rugs.
	/30	—— Operation of the Restrictive Trade Practices (Building Materials) Order 1955.
1961	/32	—— Motor spirit and motor lubricating oil.
	/34	—— Resale price maintenance in the supply and distribution of cookers and ranges.
1962-3	/35	—— Resale price maintenance in the supply and distribution of womens' nylon stockings and hand knitting yarns.

1966	/37	—— Intoxicating liquor and soft drinks.
	/38	—— Review of the operation of the Orders relating to the supply and distribution of groceries undertaken in accordance with Section 5 of the Restrictive Trade Practices (Amendment) Act 1959.
1968	/39	—— Jewellery, watches and clocks.
1970	/40	—— Bovine hides and skins.
1971	/41	—— Supply and distribution of certain electrical equipment.

Fair Trade Commission Rules:

1953	I.101/1	—— Ropes, cordage and twines.
	/2	—— Nails and screws.
	/3	—— Table ware (earthen ware and china).
	/4	—— Cutlery, spoons and forks.
	/5	—— Entry into the retail trade in petrol.
	/6	—— Electric light bulbs.
1954	/7	—— Sole leather.
	/8	—— Files and hack saw blades.
	/9	—— Dry batteries.
1955	/10	—— Carpets, carpeting and floor rugs.
	/11	—— Household textiles (non-woollen).
	/14	—— Coal.
	/15	—— Aluminium hollow ware.
1957	/18	—— Pedal bicycles, spare parts and accessories.
	/19	—— Perambulators, folding cars and sun cars.
	/21	—— Entry into the trade of the co-operative wholesale distribution of grocery goods and provisions.
	/22	—— Supply of alcoholic and non-alcoholic apple drinks, juices and concentrates to wholesalers.
1958	/23	—— Razor blades.
	/24	—— Carpets, carpeting and floor rugs.
	/25	—— Cigarettes (maintainance and resale prices by manufacturers).
1959	/28	—— Entry into the trade in the sale and/or repair of motor vehicles.
1960	/31	—— Entry into the wholesale trade in domestic electrical goods.
1961-62	/33	—— Fair Trading Rules. (Serial No.20A). (Replacing Fair Trading Rules No.20). Entry into the trade in the sale and/or repair of motor vehicles.
1962-63	/36	—— Supply of household remedies, import foods, health drinks and toilet preparations.
1954	I.102/1	Fair Trade Commission. 1st Ann. Rep. for the period ending 31st Dec. 1953. (See succeeding Ann. Reps.)
1958		Prices Act.

8 Economic Expansion and Development

(a) General Policy

1950		Industrial Development Authority Act, 1950.
1952		Undeveloped Areas Act, 1952.
1954		National Development Act, 1954.
1959		Industrial Grants Acts, 1956-9.
1957	F.53/1	Capital Investment Advisory Cttee. 1st Rep.
1958	/2	—— 2nd Rep. Pr.4406.
	/3	—— 3rd Rep. Pr.4668.

1958	F.57	Economic expansion programme. White Paper. Pr.4796.
1958	F.58	Economic development. Pr.4803.
1962	I.109	State aid to be granted to industry to enable it to meet Common Market conditions. Interim Rep. Industrial Organisation Cttee. Pr.6510.
	I.109/2	Joint export marketing. 2nd Interim Rep. I.O.C. Pr.6730.
	I.109/3	Creation of adaptation councils to promote measures of rationalisation, co-operation etc. in individual industries. 3rd Interim Rep. I.O.C. Pr.6731.
1963	I.109/7	Industrial grants. Pr.6924.
1965	I.109/24	A synthesis of reports of survey teams on twenty-two industries. I.O.C. Pr.7883.
1964	F.66/3	Measures to promote exports of manufactured goods. National Industrial Economic Council. Pr.8005
1963	F.64	Closing the gap. (Incomes and output). Pr.6957.
1963	F.65	Capital budget 1963. Pr.7048. (See succeeding papers.)
1963	F.57/1 /2 /3	Economic expansion Part I 2nd Programme. Pr.7239. Economic expansion Part II 2nd Programme. Pr.7670. Economic expansion. 2nd Programme. A Digest.
1964	A.55	Agriculture in the Second Programme for economic expansion. Pr.7697.
1964	F.66/1	Procedures for continuous review of progress under Second Programme. N.I.E.C. Pr.7794.
1964	F.66/4	Results of discussion with the industry on Second Programme targets. N.I.E.C. Pr.7987..
	F.66/2	Manpower policy. Rep. N.I.E.C. Pr.7873.
1965	I.118	Manpower policies. White Paper. Pr.8543.
1965	F.70	Administrative arrangements for implementing manpower policy. Inter-Dept. Cttee. Rep. Pr.8260.
1965	F.66/9	Administrative arrangements for implementing manpower policy. Comments on Rep. of Inter-Dept. Cttee. N.I.E.C. Pr.8475.
1964-71		For other reports on manpower, see p.44.
1965	F.71	Public capital expenditure. Pr.8562.
1965	F.57/4	Economic expansion. 2nd Programme, Progress Rep. Pr.8703.
1968	F.57/6	—— 2nd Programme. Progress Rep. for 1964-7. Pr.9949.
1968	F.66/25	Comments on 2nd Programme. Review of progress for 1964-7. N.I.E.C.
1965	F.66/7	Economic planning. N.I.E.C. Rep. Pr.8367.
1965	I.116	Development centres and industrial estates. Cttee. Rep. Pr.8461.
1965	F.66/8	Development centres and industrial estates. Cttee. Rep. N.I.E.C. Comments on the Rep. Pr.8361.
1965	F.66/10	The economic situation. 1965. N.I.E.C. Rep. No. 11. Pr.8552.
1966	F.66/14	Planning your business. N.I.E.C. Rep.

1966	F.66/15	Arrangements for planning at industry level. N.I.E.C. Rep. No. 15. Pr.8879.
1966	I.119	Progress of industrial adaptation. March 1966. Rep. Pr.8744.
1968	F.66/24	Industrial adaptation and development. N.I.E.C. Rep. No. 23. Prl.116.
1967	F.66/18	Distribution. N.I.E.C. Rep. No.17. Pr.9130.
1968	F.66/22	Change in distribution. N.I.E.C. Rep. No. 21.
1968	I.127	Grant aided industry. Survey, Oct. 1967. Prl.117.
1967	F.66/19	Full employment. Rep. No. 18. N.I.E.C. Pr.9188.
1969	F.57/7	3rd Programme. Economic and social development, 1969-72. Prl.431.
1971	F.75/4	Review of 1970 and outlook for 1971 (incorporating 3rd Programme review).
1969	F.85	Research and development in Ireland. 1967.
1969	F.66/27	Physical planning policy. N.I.E.C. Rep. No. 26. Prl. 641.
1970	F.66/28	Incomes and prices policy. N.I.E.C. Rep. No. 27. Prl. 1102.
1966	F.66/17	The work of the National Industrial Economic Council. 1963-6. Pr.9090.

Control of External Investment:

| 1934 | | Control of Manufactures Act, 1934. |
| 1958 | | Industrial Development (Encouragement of External Investment) Act, 1958. |

(b)   Some Supplementary and Statistical Papers Relating to Economic Development and Planning

1925	R.22	Economic statistics. Cttee. Rep.
1926	2/26	Statistics Bill, 1925 Seanad Sel. Cttee. R.37.
1935	I.56/1	The trend of employment and unemployment. (See succeeding Reps.)
1946	PP.26	National income and expenditure. 1938-44. White Paper. (See succeeding papers).
1964	F.59/5	Economic Statistics.
1965	F.59/6	Economic Statistics.
1963	F.65	Capital budget, 1963. (See succeeding papers.)
1965	F.66/5	Report on review of industrial progress, 1964. N.I.E.C. Rep. (See succeeding papers).
1965	F.66/6	Comments on Department of Finance review of economic progress 1964 and prospects for 1965. Pr.8521. (See succeeding ann. papers).
1965	F.66/10	The economic situation, 1965. N.I.E.C. Rep. No. 11. Pr.8552.
1967	F.75	Review of 1966 and outlook for 1967. (See succeeding papers).
1968	F.66/23	The economy in 1967 and prospects for 1968. N.I.E.C. Rep. No. 22. (See succeeding papers).
1970	U.5	Input and output tables for 1964.
1926–		Censuses of production and industrial production, 1926, 1929, 1931, 1932-5, and succeeding ann. censuses.

1933	I.78/1	Census of distribution, 1931.
1956	I.78/2	Census of distribution, 1951-54.
1962	I.78/3	Census of distribution, 1956-9.
1970	U.78/5	Census of distribution and services, 1966. Final Rep.

(c)   Particular Industries

Committee on Industrial Organisation. Reports:

1962	I.109	—— State aid to be granted to industry to enable it to meet Common Market conditions. Interim Rep. Pr.6510.
	/1	—— Cotton, linen and rayon industry. Pr.6552.
	/2	—— Joint export marketing 2nd Interim Rep. Pr.6730.
	/3	—— Creation of adaptation councils to promote measures of rationalisation, co-operation etc. in individual industries.
1962	/4	—— Leather footwear industry.
	/5	—— Paper and paper board industry.
1963	/6	—— Motor vehicle assembly industry.
	/7	—— Industrial grants. Pr.6924.
	/8	—— Fertiliser industry.
	/9	—— Shirt making industry.
	/10	—— Mantles and gowns industry.
	/11	—— Miscellaneous clothing accessories industry.
	/12	—— Wireless, television, telecommunications industry.
	/13	—— Chemicals industry.
	/14	—— Hosiery and knitwear industry.
	/15	—— Iron and steel manufactures industry.
	/16	—— Women's ready made clothing industry (other than the mantles and gowns sector).
	/17	—— Pottery, china and earthen ware industry.
	/18	—— Electrical equipment and apparatus industry.
1964	/19	—— Cocoa, chocolate and sugar confectionery and chocolate crumb industry.
	/20	—— Printing industry.
	/21	—— Paper products industry.
	/22	—— Certain aspects of redundancy. 5th Interim Rep. Pr.7846.
1965	/23	—— Wood and metal furniture industry.
	/24	—— A synthesis of reports of survey teams on twenty-two industries.
	/25	—— Leather industry.
	/26	—— Woollen and worsted industries.
	/27	—— Men's and boys' outwear clothing industry.
	/28	—— Men's protective clothing industry.
	/29	—— Agricultural machinery manufacturing industry.
	/30	—— Brushmaking industry.
	/31	—— Industrial organisation. Final Rep. Pr.8082
	/32	—— Processing of fruit and vegetables and the manufacture of jams, marmalades and other preserves etc. industry.

Committee on Industrial Progress. Reports:

1970	I.130	—— Women's outerwear.

1970	I.131	—— Fruit and vegetables processes industry.
	/1	—— Hosiery and knitwear.
	/2	—— Metal trades industry.
1971	/3	—— Paper, paper products, printing and publishing industry.
	/4	—— Tanning and dressing of leather.
	/5	—— Men's and boys' outerwear industry.
	/6	—— Electrical machinery apparatus and appliances industry.

1935   3/35   The demise of certain State mining rights. Dail Sel. Cttee. Interim Rep. (T.86).

           4/36   —— Rep. evidence (T.89).

1968   I.128   Film industry. Cttee. Rep.

1969   K.96   Metric programme for the building industry.

9 Relations with Europe

1948   X.19   European recovery programme. Basic documents and background information. P.8972. (See succeeding Reps.)

1949   X.20   European recovery programme. Ireland's long term programme 1949-53. P.9198.

1949   X.22   Working with Europe. Ireland's part in European co-operation.

1950   X.25/3   European co-operation. Agreement between the Government of Ireland and the U.S.A.

1961   F.62   European Economic Community. Pr.6106.

1962   F.61/1   European Economic Community. Developments subsequent to the White Papers 30th June 1961. Pr.6613.

1965   X.33   Free Trade Area Agreement. Pr.8623.

1966   F.66/11   Comments on the Free Trade Area Agreement. N.I.E.C. Rep.12. Pr.8610.

1967   F.76   European Communities. Pr.9283:
1. European Economic Community (EEC).
2. European Atomic Energy Community (EURATOM).
3. European Coal and Steel Community (ECSC). (April 1967).

1970   A.64   Irish Agriculture and Fisheries in the EEC. Prl.1085.

1970   F.86   Membership of the European Communities. Implications for Ireland. Prl.1110.

1972   F.95   The Accession of Ireland to the European Communities. Prl.2064.

10 Bankruptcies, Company Law, Co-operative Societies

1928   R.40/1   Private arrangements on matters relating to bankruptcies. 1st Interim Rep.

1930   R.40/2   Bankruptcy Law and the winding up of companies Amendment Cttee. Final Rep. The winding up of companies and societies, and a supplement to the 1st Interim Rep.

1958   R.88   Company Law Reform Cttee. 1958. Rep.

1963   2/63   Companies Bill 1962. Dail Special Cttee. Rep. (T.191).

1963   6/63   Companies Bill 1962. Recommittal. Dail Special Cttee. Rep. (T.195).

1963   PP.56/46   —— Official Rep. (Unrevised) of Dail Special Cttee. D.15. No.13.

1964	2/63	Companies Bill 1962. Seanad Special Cttee. Rep., procs. (T.198).
1963	3/63	Registration of business names Bill 1963. Dail Special Cttee. Rep. (T.192).
	4/63	—— Recommital. Dail Special Cttee. Rep. (T.194).
1964	I.112	Co-operative societies. Rep.

11 Industrial Assurance, Friendly Societies

1925	I.32	Industrial assurance. Cttee. Rep.
1953	PP.56/25	Friendly Societies (Amendment) Bill 1952. Dail Special Cttee. Rep. D.10.
	/26	—— Rep.
1964	7/63	Irish Estates Limited. Dail Inquiry. Inspector's Rep. (T.39)

VI FUEL AND POWER, WATER

1922	1.12	Water power resources of Ireland. Sub—Cttee. Rep. 1921.
1924	R.10/8	Water power. Rep. Jan. 1922.
1924	I.13/1	Hydro-electric scheme on the River Shannon. Correspondence between the Ministry of Industry and Commerce and Siemens-Schuckert werke, Berlin.
1925	I.13/2	The electrification of the Irish Free State. The Shannon Scheme developed by Siemens-Schuckert.
	/3	—— Reps. by experts appointed by the Government.
1924	1/24	Sligo Lighting and Electric Power Bill, 1924. Joint Cttee. Rep. PB.1.
1925	3/25	East Leinster Electricity Supply Bill, 1924. The Dublin Electricity Bill, 1924 and the Dublin and District Supply Bills, 1924. Joint Cttee. Rep. PB.7.
1929	5/29	Electricity Agreements (Adaptation) Bill, 1929. Dail Special Cttee., Rep. (T.60).
1944	I.13/4	Rural Electrification. Electricity Supply Board. Rep.
1959	R.87	Atomic energy. Cttee. Rep. 22nd May 1958.
1966	I.123	Electricity in Ireland. Scope of agreement in cross-border co-operation.
1967	I.126	Charges for electricity. Rep.
1968	V.2	Industrial relations in the Electricity Supply Board.
1936		Turf (Uses and Development) Act.
1941	I.58/2	Turf as domestic fuel. Bulletin No. 2.
	I.58/3	Irish peat waxes. Industrial Research Council.
	I.58/4	Turf as fuel for steam boilers. No. 4, Industrial Research Council.
1946	I.84	Turf development programme.
1946		Turf Development Act.

VII TRANSPORT

1 Railways

1922-25	R.2/1	Irish railways. Commission. Rep. 1922.
	/2	—— Mins. of ev. in 21 daily parts.
1924		Railways Act 1924.
1925	I.17/1	Railway Tribunal 1st Ann. Rep. 31st Dec. 1924. (See succeeding Ann. Reps.).
1925	1/25	Great Southern Railways absorption and amalgamation schemes. S.R.O. 1925 Nos. 5-8.
1926	4/26	Railways (Existing Officers and Servants) Bill. 1926. Special Rep. of Dail Special Cttee. (T.41).
1927		Railways (Road Services) Act.
1932		Railways Act [unremunerative lines].
1933		Railways Act [reduction of capital].
1941	R.70/1	Public Transport Tribunal. Inquiry. 1939. P.4866.
1944		Transport Act 1944 [amalgamation of Great Southern Railway and Dublin United Tramways into Coras Iompair Eireann].
1944	R.77/1	Dealings in Great Southern Railway stocks between 1st Jan. 1943 and 18th Nov. 1943. Tribunal Rep.
1947	I.92	Stranorlar-Glenties transport. Cttee. of Inquiry. Rep.
1949	R.70/2	Transport in Ireland, 1948. Rep. 1949 Sir James Milne.
1950		Transport Act, 1950 [amalgamation of Coras Iompair Eireann and Grand Canal Company].
1957	R.70/3	Internal transport, 1957. Cttee. Rep. Pr.4091.
1958		Transport Act, 1958. Great Northern Railway Act. 1958. [Reductions of capital and capital advances; amalgamation of Great Northern with Coras Iompair Eireann.]
1964		Transport Act.
1946	I.85	Investigation of accident on the Great Southern railway system at Straboo near Portlaoighise on 20th Dec. 1944. Rep.
1947	I.14/6	Accident on railways system of Coras Iompair Eireann 1st Aug. 1947. Inquiry Rep.
1950	I.14/7	Accident on railway system of the County Donegal railways. near Donegal on 29th Aug. 1949. Joint Cttee. Rep.

2 Canals, Inland Waterways

1923	R.3/1	Canals and inland waterways. Commission. Rep., July 1923.
	/2	—— Mins. of ev. 30 daily parts.
1950		Transport Act 1950. [Amalgamation of Grand Canal Company and Coras Iompair Eireann.]

3 Roads and Road Transport

1923	R.6	Reconditioning and improvement of roads (1923). Commission on reconstruction and development. Interim Rep.

1952	K.62	Road surfaces for animals and animal drawn traffic. Cttee. Rep.
1952	K.64	Motor Taxation Revision.
1924	3/24	Dublin United Tramways Bill, 1924. Joint Cttee. Rep. P.B.3.
1927	1/27	Dublin Tramways (Lucan Electric Railways) Bill, 1927. Joint Cttee. Rep. P.B.10.
1944		Transport Act. [Amalgamation of Dublin United Tramways and Great Southern Railway.]
1925	R.24	Taxation of road vehicles. Roads Advisory Cttee. Sub-Cttee. Interim Rep. Feb. 1925.
1928	K.3	Control and regulation of road traffic. Inter-Dept Cttee. Rep.
1955	K.68	Compensation for victims of uninsured motorists. Agreement between the Minister for Local Government and Motor Insurers Bureau.
1963	R.101	Driving while under the influence of drink or drugs. Commission. Rep.
1933		Road Transport Act, 1933. (Licensing of road transport of goods.)
1960	K.75	Proposals for road traffic legislation, 1960.
1966	I.120	Road freight transport, 1964. Sample survey.
1967	I.120/1	Road freight transport, 1964. Sample survey, Final Rep.
1968	J.28	Road Traffic Bill, 1966. Explanatory Memo.
1968		Road Traffic Act, 1968.

Donegal

| 1935 | R.53/1 | County Donegal Transport Cttee. Rep. |

4 Public Transport

| 1971 | R.113 | Defining the role of public transport in a changing environment. Rep. McKinsey. |

5 Ports

1924	2/24	State Harbours Bill, 1924. Joint Cttee. Rep. P.B.2.
1930	I.25	Port and Harbours Tribunal. Rep.
1925	2/25	Dundalk Harbour and Port Bill, 1924. Joint Cttee. Rep. P.B.6.
1926	1/26 2/26	Limerick Harbour Bill, 1926. Joint Cttee. Rep. P.B.8. —— Certain amendments. Rep. PB.9.
1931	1/31	Limerick Harbour Bill, 1930. Joint Cttee. Rep. PB.7.
1963	1/63	Limerick Harbour (Bridge) Bill, 1964. Joint Cttee. Rep. (T.190).
1929	2/29	Dublin Port and Docks (Bridge) Bill, 1927. Joint Cttee. Rep. PB.3.
1932	2/32	Cork Harbour Bill, 1932. Joint Cttee. Rep. PB.8.
1935	2/35	Galway Harbour Bill, 1933. Joint Cttee. Rep. (T.84).
1946		Harbours Act.
1964	2/64	Waterford Harbour Commissioners (Acquisition of Property) Bill, 1963. Joint Cttee. Rep. (T.199).
1962	G.16	Improvement of fishing harbour facilities in Ireland. Rep. Carl G. Bjuke.

6 Shipping

1930	X.1	Dominion legislation and merchant shipping legislation. Conference on operation. Rep. 1929.
1959	R.94	Cross channel freight rates 1959. Tribunal of Inquiry. Rep.
1924	I.14	Loss of S.S. *Lismore*. Formal investigation into the circumstances under the Merchant Shipping Act 1894. Rep. of the Court.
1943	I.14/2	Sinking of the S.S. *Moyalla*. Rep. of the Court.
1943	I.14/3	Stranding of the S.S. *Irish Plane*.
	/5	—— Report of the investigation into the loss of the *Irish Plane*.
1944	I.14/4	The loss of the pilot launch *Carraig-An-Cuain* and the examination boat no. 3 in Cork Harbour. 12th Dec. 1942. Formal Investigation.

7 Air Transport

1970	T.5	Accident to Viscount 803 aircraft, near Tuskar Rock, Co. Wexford. 24th Mar. 1968.

VIII POST OFFICE, BROADCASTING, TELEVISION

1922-25		Post Office Commission.
1922	R.5/1	—— Interim Rep.
	/2	—— —— Mins. of ev.
	/3	—— Rep. 1st Part.
	/4	—— Summary of ev.
	/5	—— Final Rep.
1924		Wireless Broadcasting. Dail Special Cttee.
	1/24	—— 1st and 2nd Interim Reps. (T.20).
	4/24	—— 3rd Interim Rep. (T.20b).
	6/24	—— Final Rep. (T.20c).
1959	R.95	Television Commission, 1959. Rep.
1964	R.104	Television Interim Rep., 1959, Gaeltacht Commission. In app. to the Commission's Final Rep., 1963
1972	I.109/72	Wireless, T.V. and tele-communications industry. Cttee. on Industrial Organisation.

IX COMMERCIAL PROPERTY, COPYRIGHT

1925	PP.49	Industrial and Commercial Property (Protection) Bill, 1925. Joint Cttee. Rep., procs.
1929		Copyright (Preservation) Act 1929.
		Merchandise marks. See p.34.
1963		Copyright Act, 1963.

X LABOUR

1 Manpower: Supply and Migration of Labour

1938	R.65/1	Seasonal migration to Great Britain 1937-8. Inter-Dept. Cttee., Rep.

1955	R.84	Emigration and other population problems 1948-54. Commission Reps. Pr.2541.
1964	F.66/2	Manpower policy. N.I.E.C. Rep. Pr.7873.
1965	I.118	Manpower policies. White Paper. Pr.8543.
1965	F.70	Administrative arrangements for administering manpower policy. Inter-Dept. Cttee. Rep. Pr.8260.
	F.66/9	—— Comments on the Rep. N.I.E.C. Pr.8475.
1967		Manpower in a developing community. Pilot survey. Drogheda. Dept. of Labour.
1968	U.4	Engineering manpower survey, 1968.
1969	V.9	Manpower in an industrial growth centre. Rep.
1971	V.10	Manpower in Galway. Rep.
1967	R.106	Supervisors. Dept. of Labour. Rep.
1968	V.4	The placement and guidance service. Institute of Public Administration. Rep.
1945	PP.25	Demobilisation and resettlement of members of the defence forces.

2 Trade Boards, Hours of Work

1922		Trade Boards Acts, 1908 and 1918. (For lists of decisions, see Stationery Office Lists.)
		Shop Hours (Drapery Trades, Dublin and Districts) Amendment Bill, 1925. Dail Special Cttee.
1925	5/25	—— Interim Rep. (T.37).
1926	1/26	—— Final Rep. (T.38).
	7/26	—— Conference of Members representing the Dail and the Seanad and certain amendments made by the Seanad. Rep. (T.44).
	4/26	—— Conference between the two Houses. Seanad Cttee. Rep. R.39.
	PP.47	—— Interim and Final Rep., Special Cttee.
1936		Night Work (Bakeries) Act, 1936.
1951	1/51	Agricultural Workers (Weekly Half-Holidays) Bill, 1950. Dail Special Cttee. Rep. (T.129).
1965	I.117	Public holidays and bank holidays. Commission of Inquiry. Rep. 1965.
1936		Conditions of Employment Act, 1936.
1936	R.61/1	Wages and conditions of service of employees in the linen and cotton industry in Saorstat Eireann. Court of Inquiry Rep.
1941	R.69/1	Dublin bakery trade. Court of Inquiry Rep.
1971	R.114	Equal Pay. Status of Women Commission. Interim. Rep.

3 Trade Unions, Industrial Relations, Labour Courts, Disputes

1941		Trade Union Act.
1942		Trade Union Act.
1942	J.56/1	Trade Union Act. Rules, 1942.

1944	R.76/1	Vocational organisation. Commission Rep., 1943.
1946		Industrial Relations Act, 1946.
1948	I.93/1	Labour Court. 1st ann. Rep., 23rd Sept. 1946 to 30th Sept. 1947. (See succeeding ann. Reps.).
1966	F.73	Rates of remuneration payable to clerical recruitment grades in the public sector of the economy. Tribunal of Inquiry. Rep.
1968	V.2	Industrial relations in the Electricity Supply Board. Cttee. Rep.
1969	V.2/1	—— Final Rep.
1969	V.5	Strikes in Bord Na Mona. Inquiry. Rep.
1969	V.6.	Disputes between F.E.U. and Maintenance Craft Unions. Rep. of Inquiry.

4 Cost of Living; Incomes Policy

1933	R.46/1	Cost of living index figure. Cttee. Rep. P.992.
1954	I.104	Household budget inquiry, 1951-2. Pr.2520.
1969	U.104/1	Household budget inquiry, 1965-6.
1962	F.64	Closing the gap (incomes and output) 1962. Pr.6957.
1970	F.66/28	Incomes and prices policy. N.I.E.C. Rep. 27. P.1102.

5 Unemployment and Redundancy

1928	R.38/1	Relief of unemployment, 1927. Cttee. 1st Interim Rep.
1928	/2	—— Final Rep.
1933		Unemployment Assistance Act.
1951	R.82	Youth unemployment. Commission. Dr J.C. McQuaid (Ch). Rep. 1951. Pr.709.
1967	F.66/19	Full employment. Rep. N.I.E.C. Pr.9188.
1964	I.109/22	Certain aspects of redundancy. Cttee. on industrial organisation. 5th Interim Rep. Pr.7846.
1967	I.125	Redundancy Payments Bill, 1967. Explanatory Memo.
1969	V.7	Redundancy Appeals Tribunal 1st Ann. Rep. Dec. 1969. (See succeeding Ann. Reps.).

6 Professions: see Education

7 International Relations

| 1963 | K.81 | Retraining and settlement in relation to the European Social Fund. |
| 1969 | V.8 | Ireland in the International Labour Organisation. Brian Hillery and Patrick Lynch. |

XI SOCIAL SECURITY

1927	R.27/3	Relief of the sick and destitute, including the insane poor. Commission Rep.
1925	R.27/1	—— Mins. of ev. 27th May 1925.
	/2	—— Mins. of ev. 2nd June 1925.

1928	R.38/1	Relief of unemployment. Cttee. 1st Interim Rep. 1927.
	/2	—— Final Rep.
1929	2/29	Poor law relief. Seanad Special Cttee. Rep. R.48
1926	R.28	Old age pension. Cttee. Rep.
1970	R.108	Care of the aged. Inter-Dept. Cttee. Rep.
1933	R.49/1	Widows and orphans pensions. Cttee Rep.
1946		Ministers and Secretaries Act [Dept. of Social Welfare estab.]
1949	K.54	Social security. Government proposals. White Paper. Oct. 1949.
1950	K.54/1	The welfare plan.
1951		Social Welfare Act 1951.
1952		Social Welfare Act 1952.
1950	K.59/1	Department of Social Welfare. 1st Rep. 22 Jan. 1947–31 Mar. 1949. (See succeeding Reps.).
1927	I.42	Workmen's compensation. Dept. Cttee. Rep.
1930	I.42/2	—— 2nd Rep.
1929	I.43/1	Workmen's compensation. Statistics 1926.
1929	2/29	Workmen's Compensation (Increase of Compensation) Bill, 1929. Dail Special Cttee. Rep.
1963	R.100	Workmen's compensation. Commission. Reps. 1962.
1967	K.92	Social Welfare. (Occupational Injuries) Act, 1966. Explanatory Memo.
1963	R.103	Itinerancy Commission Report.
1965-6		Agreement between the Government of the U.K. and the Government of the Republic of Ireland on social security (8 Feb. 1966). British Sessional Papers; 1965-6 Cmnd. 2930, xvi.

XII HEALTH

1 General: Insurance and Medical Services

1925	N.2/1	Health insurance and medical services. Cttee. Interim Rep.
	/2	—— Apps.
1927	/3	—— Final Rep.
1927	N.27	National Health Insurance (International Agreements) Bd. Rep. to the National Health Insurance Joint Cttee. and to the Irish Commissioners.
1929	N.1/2	Administration of the national health insurance in all Ireland. Rep. of 1/4/21–31/3/22, Saorstat Eireann from 1/4/22–31/3/28 National Health Insurance Commission.
1930	K.29	Conference between Depts. of Local Government and Health and representatives of local Public Health and Assistance Authorities, 1930.
1933	1/33	National Health Insurance Bill 1933. Seanad Select Cttee. Rep. R.54.

1946		Ministers and Secretaries Act. [Dept. of Health estb.].
1951	K.60/1	Dept. of Health 1st Rep. See succeeding Ann. Reps.
1947	K.51	Health services. Outline of the proposals for the improvement of of the health services. White Paper.
1952	K.63	Proposals for an improved and extended health service. July 1952.
1956	K.72	Voluntary health insurance scheme. Rep. of advisory body.
1957		Voluntary Health Insurance Act.
1953	K.65/1	Health progress 1947-53.
1962	2/62	Health services. Sel. Cttee. Interim Rep. (T.186).
1963	1/63	—— 2nd Interim Rep. (T.189).
1966	K.87	Health services and their future development.
1964	K.71/1	Maternity and Child Welfare Services (Amendment) Regulations 1964. Form of agreement with medical practitioners.
1968	Z.2	The child health services.

2 Hospitals

1923	6/23	Public Charitable Hospitals (Temporary Provisions) Bill 1923. Dail Special Cttee. Rep. (T.12).
1930	2/30	Public Charitable Hospitals (Temporary Provisions) Bill 1929. Dail Special Cttee. Rep. (T.64).
	3/30	—— Bill re-committed. Special Cttee. Rep. (T.66).
1931	2/31	—— No.2 Bill 1931. Special Cttee. Rep. (T.72).
	3/31	—— —— No.3 Bill 1931. (T.73).
1932	3/32	Public Charitable Hospitals (Amendment) Bill 1932. Dail Special Cttee. Rep. (T.75).
1936	R.56/1	Hospitals Commission. 1st General Rep. 1933-4.
1938	R.56/2	—— 2nd General Rep. 1935 and 1936.
1939	/3	—— 3rd General Rep.
1942	/4	—— 4th General Rep.
1943	/5	—— 5th General Rep.
1946	/6	—— 6th General Rep.
1950	/7	—— 7th General Rep.
1936	2/36	National Maternity Hospital Dublin. (Charter Amendment) Bill, 1936. Joint Cttee. Rep. (T.88).
1950	K.45	Dublin fever hospital. Correspondence relating to the removal from office of members of the Board. Rep.
	K.45/1	Dublin fever hospital Board. Sworn inquiry Nov. 1944, into the performance of their duties. Mins. of ev.
1951	2/51	Meath Hospital Bill, 1950. Dail Sel. Cttee. Rep. (T.130).
1953	1/53	Royal Hospital for Incurables, Dublin. Charter (Amendment) Bill, 1952. Joint Cttee. Seanad Rep. (T.137).
1953	1/53	Sir Patrick Dunn's Hospital Bill, 1953. Joint Cttee. Oireachtas Rep. (T.146).
1968	Z.1	Outline of the future hospital system. Rep. of the Consultative Council on the General Hospital Services.

3 Particular Problems

1922-25	M.5	Tuberculosis in Ireland. 1908.
1946	K.46	Tuberculosis. Dept. of Local Government and Health.
1947	K.49	Mental Treatment Act, 1945. Memo for Public Assistance Authorities and their officers.
1960	K.76	The problem of the mentally handicapped.
1965	K.84	Mental handicap. Commission Rep.
1967	K.90	Mental illness. Commission Rep. 1966.
1962	K.80	Incidence of dental caries in school children and an analysis of public piped water supplies. Dublin, Kildare, Wicklow. Rep.
	K.80/1	—— Cork, Limerick, Waterford. Rep.
1962-63	/2	—— Louth, Wexford, Galway, Laoighis. Rep.
1964	/3	—— Tipperary (N. Riding), Tipperary (S. Riding), Kilkenny, Carlow. Rep.
	/4	—— Kerry, Clare, Westmeath and Offaly. Rep.
1965	/5	—— Health. (Fluoridation of Water Supplies) Act 1960.
	/6	—— Roscommon, Longford, Leitrim, Cavan and Monaghan. Rep.
1958	R.90	Fluorine Consultative Council. Rep.
1960	R.98	Radioactivity Consultative Council. Rep.
1961	K.77	Radioactive fall-out in Ireland in 1960. Study.

4 Food Purity, Nutrition

1924	K.5	A bacteriological investigation of Dublin milks. 1921. J.W. Bigger. M.D.,D.P.H.
1949	K.53/1	Methods of dietary survey and results from Dublin investigation. National nutrition survey. Pt.I.
	/2	Survey of the congested districts. Pt.II.
1950	/3	—— Large and small towns. Pt.III.
	/4	—— Farming families. Pt.IV.
	/5	—— Farm workers' families. Pt.V.
1951	/6	—— Dietary survey of exceptional rural families and summarised results of all dietary surveys with apps. Pt.VI.
	/7	—— Clinical survey. Pt.VII.
	/8	—— Complete reports of dietary and clinical surveys. Pt.I to Pt.VI
1954	I.104	Household Budget Inquiry. 1951-2.
1969	U.104/1	Household Budget Inquiry. 1965-6.
1961	Z.9	Education and Training in hygiene and food hygiene. Food hygiene Cttee. Rep.

5 Pharmaceutical Products, Drugs

1949	I.58/5	Manufacture of formalin. Emergency Scientific Research Bureau.
1957	I.101/20	Supply and distribution of proprietary and patent medicines and infant foods and medical and toilet preparations. Inquiry into the conditions. Fair Trade Commission. Rep.
1971	R.111	Drug abuse. Working party. Rep.

6 Burial Grounds

1933	1/33	Dublin General Cemeteries Bill, 1933. Joint Cttee. Rep. PB. 9.

| 1966 | 1/66 | Huguenot Cemetery Dublin (Peter Street) Bill, 1965. Joint Cttee. Rep. (T.205). |
| 1970 | 4/70 | Dublin Cemeteries Cttee. Bill 1969. Joint Cttee. Rep. Procs. (T.222). |

7 Professions

For Papers on Dentists, Surgeons and Apothecaries, see Education: Professions.

XIII HOUSING AND TOWN PLANNING

1 Rent Control, Landlord, Tenant

1923	J.1	Increase of Rent and Mortgage Interest (Restrictions) Act, 1920. Dept. Cttee. Reps. (Mar. 1923).
	J.2	—— Rules, 1923.
1927	R.35/1	Town Tenants Commission, 1927; working of the Small Dwellings Acquisition Act, 1899. Interim Rep., apps.
1928	/2	—— Final Rep., apps.
1941	R.71/1	Town Tenants (Occupation Tenancies) Tribunal. Rep.
1954	J.62/1	Rent control. Rents and Leasehold Commission. Rep.
1954	J.62/2	Reversionary leaseholds under the Landlord and Tenants Acts. Rent and Leaseholds Commission. Rep.
1964	J.68	Ground Rents. Rep.
1967	J.74	Landlord and Tenants (Ground Rents) Bill, 1965 as passed by both Houses of the Oireachtas. Explanatory Memo.
1967	J.76	Rent Restrictions (Amendment) Act. Explanatory Memo.
1967	J.79	Occupational tenancies under the Landlord and Tenant Act, 1931.
1968	J.81	Questions arising under the Landlord and Tenant Act, 1958-67. Landlord and Tenant Commission. Rep.

2 Housing: Conditions and Programme; County Homes

1944	R.75/1	Housing of the working classes of the City of Dublin, 1939-43.
1945	I.82/1	Post-war building programme.
1948	K.52	Housing. A review of past operations and immediate requirements. White Paper.
1949	K.55	Ireland is building.
1964	K.82	Housing. Progress and prospects.
1967	K.94	Your development plan.
1967	K.95	A house of your own.
1969	K.97	Housing in Ireland.
1969	K.98	Housing in the seventies.
1951	K.61	Reconstruction and improvement of county homes.
1969	K.96	Metric programme for the building industry.
1933	R.47/1	Sale of cottages and plots. Commission. Rep.

3 House Design

A number of Papers, circulars etc. were issued for guidance of authorities, associations etc. providing houses, on design, layout, specifications etc. See Stationery Office Catalogues.

4 Town and Regional Planning

1929	3/29	Town Planning Bill, 1929. Seanad Sel. Cttee. Rep. R.49.
1934		Town and Regional Planning Act, 1934.
1934	K.34/1	Town and Regional Planning Act, 1934. Summary of provisions.
1965	K.83	Planning and Development Act, 1963. Explanatory Memo.
1965	K.85	The Dublin region. Preliminary Rep. Myles Wright.
1967	K.85/1	—— Advisory regional plan and Final Rep. Part I.
	/2	—— Final Rep., Part II.
1966	K.88	The Limerick region. The Rep. and advisory outline plan.
1968	K.88/2	—— Advisory Cttee., Plan Vol.II with additional material from Vol.I. Rep.
1967	K.94	Your development plan.

XIV A EDUCATION

1 General Policy

1926	M.15	National programme conference. Rep. and programme presented to the Minister for Education.
1966	E.56	Investment in education. Rep. of survey team appointed by the Minister for Education. Professor P.K. Lynch. Pr.8311.
	E.56/1	—— Annexes and appendices.
1966	F.66/16	Comments on *Investment in Education*. N.I.E.C.

2 Primary and Secondary Education

1922-25	R1/1	Primary Education. Vice-Regal Cttee. Ireland 1913.
	/3	Mins. of ev. See also British Sessional Papers. Primary education (Ireland) System of inspection. Vice-Regal Cttee. Final Rep; 1914 Cd.7235,xxviii, 1081. Mins. of ev. etc.; 1913 Cd.6829, xxii, 235. 1914 Cd.7229, Cd.7480, xxxviii,5.
1927	EP.1	Inspection of primary schools. Cttee. Rep.
1936	R.58/1	Raising the school leaving age. Inter-Dept. Cttee. Rep.
1954	E.28/2	The primary school. Council for Education. Rep.
1961	E.28/3	Curriculum in the secondary schools. Council for Education Rep.
1964	R.104	Provision of text books in Irish for secondary schools. 1st Interim Rep. 1959 Gaeltacht Commission. Rep. in apps. to Final Rep. 1963.

3 Higher Education

1967	E.59	Higher Education. Presentation and summary of Rep. of the Commission, 1960-67.
	/1	—— II. Rep. Vol.I. Chapters 1-19.
1968	/2	—— 2nd Rep. Vol.II.

1969	E.66	Higher Education Authority. 1st Ann. Rep. 1968-9. (See succeeding Ann. Reps.).
1971	E.72	Submissions to Higher Education Authority. Comhairle na Gaeilge.

4 Technical Education

1932	A.1/10	Department of Agriculture and Technical Instruction for Ireland. 29th and Final General Rep. 1930-31.
1927	R.39	Technical education. Commission Rep.
1930		Vocational Education Act.
1967	R.106	Supervisors. Dept. of Labour. Rep.
1969	E.65	Establishment of a board which would award national qualifications at technical and technological levels. Initial recommendation by the Higher Education Authority. Memo.A.

5 Adult Education

1970	E.69	National adult education survey. Interim Rep.

6 Teachers: Training, Salaries

1970	E.67	Teacher education. Higher Education Authority. Rep.
1926	E.I.2/4	Teachers' salaries grant, 1923-4: Rep. of the Intermediate Education Commissioners as to the application.
1926	E.I.2/5	Teachers' salaries grant 1924-5: Rep. of the Minister for Education under the Intermediate Education (Ireland) Act, 1914.
1949	R.80	National teachers' salaries etc. 1949. Cttee. Rep., apps. Judge Patrick J. Roe, S.C. *Ch.*
1960	R.99	Teachers' Salaries Cttee. Rep., apps. Presented to the Minister for Education, 29th July 1960.
1968	E.61	Teachers' salaries. Tribunal Rep. Presented to the Minister for Education.

7 Special Problems

1936	R.59/1	Reformatory and industrial school system, 1934-6. Commission Rep.
1970	E.68	Reformatory and industrial schools system. Rep.
1960	K.76	The problem of the mentally handicapped.
1969	K.84	Mental handicap. Commission of Inquiry. Rep.
1969	E.63	Special education in Ireland.
1971	E.70	Education facilities for the children of itinerants.

8 Universities, Professions

1924	E.1	Irish Universities Act 1908. App. to the Final Rep. of the Dublin Commissioners.
1940		Institute of Advanced Studies Act.
1959	R.93	Accommodation needs of the constituent colleges of the National University of Ireland. Commission Rep.
1924	4/24	Apothecaries' Hall, Dublin Bill 1924. Joint Cttee. Rep. PB.4.

1928	2/28	Legal Practitioners (Qualification) Bill 1928. Dail Special Cttee. Rep. (T.52).
1928	PP.56/1	Dentists Bill, 1927. Cttee. Rep.
	/2	—— 3rd and 4th schedules.
	/3	—— 2nd Rep.
1960	1/60	Institution of Civil Engineers in Ireland (Charter Amendment) Bill, 1959. Joint Cttee. Rep., procs. (T.171).
1969	1/68	Institution of Civil Engineers of Ireland (Charter Amendment) Bill 1968. Joint. Cttee. Oireachtas. Rep. (T.217).
1965	4/64	Royal College of Surgeons in Ireland (Charter Amendment) Bill 1964. Joint Cttee. Rep. (In *Dail reps.*).
1966	3/66	Institute of Chartered Accountants in Ireland (Chartered Amendment) Bill 1965. Joint Cttee. Rep. (In *Dail reps.*) (T.206).

XIV B   NATIONAL CULTURE

1 The Gaeltacht

1926-28	R.23/27	Gaeltacht Commission Rep.
	R.23/1-	
	23/24	—— Mins. of ev. 17th April to 21st Sept. 1925. 24 days ev.
	R.23/25	—— Statement from Government Departments not embodied with the relative oral evidence.
	R.23/26	—— Persons who were not examined before the Commission. Statements of evidence.
1928	R.23/28	—— Statement of Government policy on recommendations of the Commission.
1964	R.102	An Comisiun um Athbheochan na Gaeilge. Summary in English of Final Rep. 13 July, 1963.
1964	R.104	An Comisiun um Athbheochan na Gaeilge. An Tuarascail Dheiridh.
1965	R.105	Restoration of the Irish language. White Paper.
1929-67		Housing (Gaeltacht) Acts.
1949-54		Alginate Industries (Ireland) (Acquisition of Shares) Act, 1949-1954.
1956		Ministers and Secretaries (Amendment) Act, 1965. [Dept. of the Gaeltacht estb.].
1957-68		Gaeltacht Industries Acts.
1969	F.74/1	Comhlacht Comhairleach na Gaeilge. Tuarascail don Treimhse 1 Aibrean, 1966 go dti 14 Meitheamh, 1968.
1971	F.93/2	Local Government and Development Institutions for the Gaeltacht. Comhairle na Gaeilge.

2 The Irish Language

1965	R.105	Restoration of the Irish Language. White Paper.
1966	/1	—— Progress Rep. 31st Mar. 1966. White Paper.
1969	/2	—— Progress Rep. 31st Mar. 1968. White Paper.

1964		Provision of text books in Irish for secondary schools. Interim Rep., 1959 in apps. to Gaeltacht Commission Final Rep., 1963.
1969	F.80	A view of the Irish language.
1971	F.93/1	Towards a language policy. Comhairle na Gaeilge.
1971	E.72	Submissions to the Higher Education Authority. Comhairle na Gaeilge.

3 Historical Manuscripts, the Arts

1923	9/23	Irish manuscripts. Seanad Cttee. Rep. (R.11).
1924	8/24	—— Final Rep. (R.22).
1953	M.60	Report on arts in Ireland. Professor T. Bodkin.
1952	E.43	Ancient objects in bogs and farmlands.
1956	M.65	Hugh Lane and his pictures. T. Bodkin.
1967	E.58	Council of Design. Rep.

4 Broadcasting and Television

1924	1/24	Wireless broadcasting. Dail Special Cttee. 1st and 2nd Interim Reps. (T.20).
	4/24	—— 3rd Interim Rep. (T.20b).
	6/24	—— Final Rep. (T.20c).
1959	R.95	Television Commission, 1959. Rep.
1964	R.104	Television. Interim Rep. 1959, in apps. to Gaeltacht Commission's Final Rep., 1963.

XV POPULATION

1938	R.65/1	Seasonal migration to Britain, see p.43.
1955	R.84	Emigration and other population problems. Commission. 1948-54. Pr.2541.

Censuses of Population taken in 1926, 1936, 1941, 1943, 1946, 1951, 1956, 1961, and 1966. For details of the published volumes, see Stationery Office Catalogues.

XVI INTOXICATING LIQUOR CONTROL, RACING, BETTING

1922-25	R.21/18 /1 to 17	Intoxicating Liquor Commission. Rep.
		—— Mins. of ev. 17 days ev. (R.21/9). Mins. of ev. with app. by Sir Thomas Callan Macardle, K.B.E. 18th May, 1925.
1924	15/24	Intoxicating Liquor (General) Bill, 1924. Conference of members representing the Seanad and Dail on certain amendments made by the Seanad. Dail Rep. (T.32).
1930	R.21/19	Intoxicating Liquor Commission, 1929. Rep. of the reconstituted Commission.
1943	1/43	Conference between Members of the Dail and the Seanad on amendments No.1 and No.2 by the Seanad to the Intoxicating Liquor Bill, 1942, together with proceedings of the Conference. Oireachtas Rep.

1958	R.86	Laws relating to the supply of intoxicating liquor 1957. Commission, Reps.
1957	I.101/22	Supply of alcoholic and non-alcoholic apple drinks, juices and concentrates to wholesalers. Fair Trading Commission. Rules, No.17.
1966	I.101/37	Intoxicating liquor and soft drinks. Rep. Fair Trading Commission.
1966	I.122/1	Brewing prices inquiry.
1948	R.79	Allegations relative to the sale of Locke's distillery. Tribunal of Inquiry set up pursuant to a resolution passed by the House of the Oireachtas, Rep.
1928	F.28	Irish racing. Inter-Dept. Cttee. Rep.
1929	5/29	Betting Act 1926 and the law relating to the business of bookmaking. Joint Cttee. Interim Rep. (T.56).
	6/29	—— Report. (T.58).
1932	R.45/1	Issue of totaliser licences for greyhound racing tracks. Cttee. Rep.
1952	A.39	Greyhound industry. Advisory Cttee. Rep.

XVII LEGAL ADMINISTRATION, POLICE, LAW

1 Administration and Procedure

1924	R.4	Judiciary Cttee. 1923. Rep.
1926	5/26	Rules of Court. Seanad Special Cttee. Rep. R.40.
1928	PP.60	Rules of Circuit Court. Joint Cttee. Rep.
1926	3/26	Coroners Bill, 1925. Seanad Sel. Cttee. Rep. R.38.
1930	4/30	Courts of Justice Act, 1924. Joint Cttee. Rep. Procs., apps. (T.69).
1962	J.66	Programme of Law Reform. Pr.6379.

Court Practices and Procedure. Committee. Interim Reports:—

1964	J.67	—— 1st Rep.	Indictable offences.
1965	J.70	—— 2nd Rep.	Jury service.
1966	J.71	—— 3rd Rep.	Jury trial in civil actions.
		—— 4th Rep.	Jury challengers.
	/1	—— 5th Rep.	Increase in jurisdiction of the District Court and the Circuit Court.
1967	/2	—— 6th Rep.	The criminal jurisdiction of the High Court.
	/3	—— 7th Rep.	Appeals from conviction and indictment.
1969	/4	—— 8th Rep.	Service of the court documents by post. Fees of professional witnesses.
1970	/5	—— 9th Rep.	Proof of previous convictions.
1971	/6	—— 10th Rep.	Interest rates and judgement debts.
1972	/7	—— 11th Rep.	

1967	J.77	Criminal Procedure Bill, 1965. (Enacted as the Criminal Procedure Act, 1967). Explanatory Memo.
1957	2/57	Statute of Limitations Bill, 1954. Seanad Special Cttee. Rep.
1953	1/53	Judicial salaries: expense allowances, pensions. Dail Sel. Cttee. Rep. (T.140).

2 Police

1928	J.34	Coughlan shooting inquiry. Tribunal. Rep.
1932	J.49/1	Kilrush, County Clare. Rep. of sworn inquiry 7th-10th Sept. 1932.
1968	J.80	Death of Liam O'Mahony. Tribunal appointed by the Minister of Justice, July 19th 1967.
1970	R.109	Remuneration and conditions of service. Commission on the Garda Siochana, Rep. (Conroy Rep.).

3 Prisons

1929	J.4/8	General Prisons Board. Ann. Rep. 1927-8. (See succeeding Ann. Reps.)
		Prison Closing Orders:
1929-31	J.9/1	—— Kilkenny, 1929.
	/2	—— Kilmainham, 1929.
	/3	—— Dundalk, 1931.

4 Juvenile Offenders

| 1936 | R.59/1 | Reformatory and industrial schools system, 1934-6. Commission Rep. |
| 1970 | E.68 | Reformatory and industrial schools system. Rep. |

5 Law

1935	1/35	Criminal Law Amendment Bill, 1934. Seanad Special Cttee. Rep. (R.58).
1958	3/58	Law Reform (Personal Injuries) Bill, 1957. Dail Special Cttee. Rep. (T.166).
1965	J.69	Malicious injuries. Inter-Dept. Cttee. Summary of Rep.
1942	2/42	Law of Torts (Miscellaneous Reforms) Bill, 1940-1. Dail Cttee. Rep.
1961	1/61	Civil Liability Bill, 1960. Special Cttee. Rep. (T.180).
1962	PP.56/31	Civil Liability Bill, 1960. D.13 Special Cttee. Rep.
	/32	—— Official Rep. (Unrevised). Special Cttee. Rep. D.13 No.2.
	/33	—— Rep. Special Cttee. D.13.
1926	PP.23	Bodies Corporate (Executors) Bill, 1928. Sel. Cttee. Rep.
1966	J.72	Succession Act, 1965. Explanatory Memo.
1967	J.78	Registration of Title Bill, 1964. Explanatory Memo.
1925	J.1	Increase of Rent and Mortgage Interest (Restrictions) Act 1920. Dept. Cttee. Reps. (Mar. 1923).
1924	J.2	—— Rules, 1923.
1927	R.35/1	Town Tenants Commission, 1927; working of the Small Dwellings Acquisition Act, 1899. Interim Rep., apps.
1928	/2	—— Final Rep., apps.
1941	R.71/1	Town Tenants (Occupation tenancies) Tribunal. Rep.
1954	J.62/1	Rent control. Rents and Leaseholds Commission, Rep.
	/2	—— Reversionary leaseholds and Landlord and Tenant Acts. Rents and Leaseholds Commission Rep.

1964	J.68	Ground rents. Rep.
1967	J.74	Landlord and Tenants. (Ground Rents) Bill, 1965 as passed by both Houses. Explanatory Memo.
1967	J.79	Occupational tenancies under the Landlord and Tenant Act, 1931.
1968	J.81	Questions arising under the Landlord and Tenant Acts 1958-67. Landlord and Tenant Commission.

1930	5/30	Legitimacy Bill, 1929. Dail Special Cttee. Rep. (T.68).
1931	2/31	—— Seanad Special Cttee. Rep. R.53.
1932	J.48/1	Illegitimate Children (Affiliation Orders) Act, 1930. Rules 1931.

| 1971 | R.114 | Status of women. Commission. Interim Rep. on equal pay. |

| 1963 | R.101 | Driving whilst under the influence of drink or a drug. Commission Rep. |
| 1955 | K.68 | Compensation for victims of uninsured motorists (in respect of injury to person) together with some notes on its scope and purpose. Motor Insurers' Bureau of Ireland. Text of agreement with the Minister of Local Government providing for a scheme. |

6 Censorship

| 1927 | R.34 | Evil literature. Cttee. Rep. |
| 1927-67 | | Censorship of Publications Acts, 1927, 1929, 1946, 1967. |

7 Fire Protection, Summertime

1935	R.62/1	Fire at Pearse Street, Dublin. Tribunal Rep.
1943	R.74/1	Fire at St. Joseph's Orphanage, Cavan. Tribunal Rep.
1966	K.89	Fire protection for hotels.
1967	K.91	Fire protection standards. Mar. 1967.
1941	R.72/1	Summertime. Cttee. Rep. 1941.

8 Civil Order, Public Safety, Emergency Powers

1924	D.3	General regulations as to the trial of civilians by military courts, made by the Army Council, 2nd Oct. 1922.
1923	28/23	Public Safety (Emergency Powers) Act, 1923.
1923	29/23	Public Safety (Emergency Powers) Act, No. 2, 1923.
1925	17/25	Fire Arms Act, 1925.
1925	10/25	Fire Arms (Temporary Provisions) (Continuance) Act, 1925.
1924	J.5/1	Regulations made pursuant to Section 8 of the Public Safety (Emergency Powers) Act, 1923 (Licenses for firearms).
1924	J.5/2.	Regulations made under Section 7 of the Public Safety (Powers of Arrest and Detention) Temporary Act, 1924.
1939		Treason Act.
1939		Offences Against the State Act.
1940		Offences Against the State (Amendment) Act, 1940.

APPENDIX

Reports of the National Industrial Economic Council

In the foregoing List, the Reports of the National Industrial Economic Council are necessarily mingled with those of other bodies and departments on related topics. The following list, unencumbered by the papers of other agencies, makes it possible to view its work as a whole.

1964	F.66	Economic expansion. Interim Rep. on 2nd programme.
	/1	Procedures for continuous review of progress under the 2nd programme.
	/2	Manpower Policy.
	/3	Measures to promote exports of manufactured goods.
	/4	Results of discussions with industry on the 2nd programme targets.
1965	/5	Review of industrial progress 1964.
	/6	Comments on Dept. of Finance review of economic progress in 1964 and prospects for 1965.
	/7	Economic planning.
	/8	Comments on report of Committee on Development Centres and Industrial Estates.
	/9	Comments on Rep. of Inter-Dept. Committee on Administrative arrangements for implementing manpower policy.
	/10	Economic situation, 1965.
1966	/11	Comments on Free Trade Area Agreement.
	/12	Comments on Dept. of Finance review of economic progress in 1965 and prospects for 1966.
	/13	Review of industrial progress 1965.
	/14	Planning your business.
	/15	Arrangements for planning at industry level.
	/16	Comments on 'Investment in Education'.
	/17	The work of the National Industrial Economic Council 1963-66.
1967	/18	Distribution.
	/19	Full employment.
	/20	Review of industrial progress 1966.
	/21	Comments on Dept. of Finance Rep., review of 1966 and outlook for 1967.
1968	/22	Change in distribution. Rep. No.21.
	/23	Economy in 1967 and prospects for 1968. Rep. No.22.
	/24	Industrial adaptation and development. Rep. No.23.
	/25	Comments on 2nd programme, review of progress 1964-67. Rep. No.24.
1969	/26	The economy in 1968 and the prospects for 1969.
	/27	Physical planning. Rep. No. 26.
1970	/28	Incomes and prices policy. Rep. No. 27.
	/29	The economy in 1969 and the prospects for 1970. Rep. No. 28.

INDEX

This brief index is designed to assist readers to find individual papers. It is based on the key word or words of the title. Where this is identical with the main subject heading, no separate entry has been made. The names of the personal authors and chairmen given in the text are also included.